Why People Make No Sense

(Until They Do)

Christine Kuca-Thompson,
Greg Barnes, David Koutsoukis

Copyright © 2025

The moral right to be identified as the creators of the work has been asserted by them in accordance with the Copyright, Designs and Patents Act 1988. All rights reserved.

No part of this book may be reproduced, stored in a retrieval system or transmitted in any form or by any means, electronic, mechanical, photocopying, recording or otherwise, without the prior permission of the authors.

Book Cover by Ven Visual

Book formatting design by Red Feather Publishing

Second edition 2025

Print ISBN: 978-1-7644310-2-6

E-book ISBN: 978-1-7644310-1-9

Contents

Foreword	2
Introduction	4
The Origin and Evolution of the Click! Colours	9
The Story	14
1. Successful People Understand People!	16
1st Piece of Gold	19
2. People Are Different!	20
2nd Piece of Gold	24
3. Diversity Impacts on the Workplace	25
3rd Piece of Gold	31
4. Diversity Impacts on the Home	32
4th Piece of Gold	45
5. Great Relationships and Teamwork Don't 'Just Happen'	46
5th Piece of Gold	51

Checkpoint 1	52
6. Everyone Has Four Sub-Personalities	54
6th Piece of Gold	62
Click! Colours Sub-Personalities Summary	63
Checkpoint 2	64
7. Some Sub-Personalities 'Shine' Brighter than Others	67
Checkpoint 3	73
7th Piece of Gold	75
8. Use the Click! Colours to Understand Others	76
8th Piece of Gold	80
Checkpoint 4	81
9. Beware of Stereotyping and Generalisations	83
9th Piece of Gold	91
10. External Factors Also Influence Behaviour	92
10th Piece of Gold	98
11. How We See Ourselves Is Not How Others See Us	99
11th Piece of Gold	103
12. Successful People Know Themselves and Apply This Knowledge	104
Checkpoint 5	110
Checkpoint 6	117

12th Piece of Gold	121
13. Use Click! Colours to Boost Success	122
13th Piece of Gold	139
14. Use the Click! Colours to Enhance Relationships at Home	140
14th Piece of Gold	155
15. Use the Click! Colours to Build Quality Workplace Relationships	156
15th Piece of Gold	169
16. Use Click! Colours to Improve Your Life	170
Checkpoint 7	181
16th Piece of Gold	183
The Single Most Important Lesson	184
17. The Pot of Gold at the End of the Rainbow	187
18. The Final Piece of Gold	191
What's Next?	192
Facilitator Resources	194
Products and Services	196
About the Original Authors	207
About the Contributors	208

There's a pot of gold at the end of the rainbow.

You just have to know how to find it!

Discovering simple yet powerful ways to boost success and happiness is like finding the proverbial pot of gold at the end of the rainbow.

This book provides the knowledge, techniques and tools that create success in relationships, teamwork, decision making, leadership, careers, wealth creation, friendships, partnerships, parenting, and personal wellbeing.

So, relax and enjoy this enthralling journey as you discover how to build exceptional relationships, reduce stress and get more out of life.

Foreword

I first came across Click! Colours about 20 years ago through my friendship with the creators and authors, Greg Barnes and David Koutsoukis. At that time, I was running my own training business and soon realised that Click! Colours would be a beneficial addition to our range. I added it to our influencing program, customer service program, and projects program so people could get a better idea of how they work as a team.

I then had the opportunity to buy into Click! Colours and become Greg's silent partner. I knew the benefits that Click! Colours could bring to organisations and people, and with so much potential, it was not a hard decision. In a complex world where time is of the essence, this tool is very time-effective, lots of fun, and a more cost-effective tool compared to other personality and psychometric tools on the market. It helps people build self-awareness, empathy, understanding, improves communication, and helps everyone work better as a team. Click! Colours is perfectly positioned to do this. As the current sole owner of Click! Colours International, Greg was a friend, fun to be around, someone to bounce around crazy ideas with, plus a bit of a business mentor to me. His original book, *The Genie Within*, was the starting point for what we now know as Click! Colours.

This book is a story about a fictional company that transitions from one of misunderstanding and conflict to a greater understanding and emotional intelligence through the introduction of Click! Colours.

We have made some minor changes to the book to make it more current, but the story is unchanged.

It is really, really powerful. I have found that people who have experienced Click! Colours love the book. It is exciting that the book has some added insight from people new to Click! Colours. The feedback is really positive, and I hope you enjoy the story and the characters.

•••• Andy Buchanan-Hughes

Owner, Click! Colours International

Introduction

Have you ever met someone that you CLICKED with right away? And others you found frustrating or annoying? It makes you question why some people make no sense.

This fun and informative book reveals a simple yet powerful formula to explain why people behave the way they do. It will help you understand why you CLICK! with some people and CLASH with others.

We often do not get to choose who is on our team, in our family, or in our social circle. To build good relationships, we need to understand the behaviour of the people we live and work with.

Relationships are all around us and are the foundation of all achievement. Think of all the people you have met or interacted with in the past week. We need good relationships to be a good coach, parent, manager, leader, partner, workmate, teacher, salesperson, family member, colleague, friend, or acquaintance. Positive relationships help us to achieve our goals. They help us to work together as a team, run a successful business, have a career, and so on.

Numerous research studies[1] have found that good relationships positively impact our happiness levels. The more satisfied we are with our relationships, the happier we are. This is why many of our good memories involve experiences with other people. And why a bad day can stay with us much longer than a good day. We naturally try to figure out what went wrong, what we could have done differently, or why some people behave the way they do.

There have been dozens, if not hundreds, of personality models, tools, and concepts. They each aimed to explain why people behave the way they do. I have completed many personality surveys either for my own interest, or as part of my work or studies. I enjoyed reading the reports that told me 'Who I was' but there were often parts that did not apply to me. And even though they were helpful at the time, I cannot remember what numbers or letters labelled me, or how I would understand other people without reading their personal report.

When I was introduced to Click! Colours it all made sense. The power of Click! Colours lies in its simplicity. Instead of dozens of questions, computer logins, prework, debriefings, expensive fees, or complicated reports, Click! Colours use four simple cards.

They are effective because they are easy to access, easy to use and easy to understand.

---

1. https://community.thriveglobal.com/relationships-happiness-well-being-life-lessons/

As busy people, it is the simple things that work the best (or shine the brightest). Although the cards are simple, they are powerful. They make the complex simple. Designed over several years by analysing different personality models and tools, Click! Colours took the best to create a tool that is effective, user-friendly and easy to use.

The Self-Discovery approach enabled me to discover which one was most like me. It allowed me to discover that in some situations, I am more like some of the other styles. This insight helped me understand myself and others better. Click! Colours gave me the tools to adjust my approaches based on the characteristics showing at the time.

Here is a short example. I really enjoy planning, organising and making sure everything is right. When you read the book, you will understand that I am a true Green. My business partner is the ideas person, always coming up with a new idea, or new approach and you will see she is a Yellow. Typically, we clash. But since bringing Click! Colours into our business, we complement rather than clash.

I keep the cards on my desk and reflect on them when I want to send her an email with lots of information and questions. She reflects on the cards when she needs to pitch an idea to me. For our business, we have found the perfect way of working; Jennifer has the ideas, and I bring them to fruition. And together we have delivered Click! Colours workshops to thousands of people.

This book introduces you to our four characters, representing each of the four cards, as they explore themselves and others through the Click! Colours journey.

They build their emotional intelligence through recognising the diverse strengths everyone brings and the challenges that are present in the style that is least like them.

I invite you to discover Click! Colours and how it can change the way you approach personal and professional relationships. Originally written in 2008, this revised version has been modernised, with the story and characters remaining true to the original book.

The book starts with co-creator David Koutsoukis giving an overview of the origin and evolution of the Click! Colours tool and methodology. He provides a rationale and a set of criteria that was used for the development of the Click! Colours and outlines its advantages, making sure Click! Colours is faster, better, cheaper and easier than other personality tools.

Then the story begins. You will meet our four colourful characters and see them reflected in yourself, your colleagues, friends and family. The insight you gain from the characters will help you see the world through the eyes of people who are different to you, those same people who can be frustrating and annoying. This will help you understand why and how to Click! better with those that are not like you.

As humans, we learn by recognising, labelling and predicting the patterns of behaviour of the people we live and work with – so you can respond to those patterns in a way that helps you maintain positive relationships with them.

This book is designed to help you learn and grow. If you read something that resonates, highlight it, dog-ear the page, or post-it note it. Use it, reflect on it, and read it again. We want your book to look well-read and well-used.

If you are a facilitator who will be delivering Click! Colours workshops, this book will give you a deeper insight into the four characters and the workshop approach. There are so many nuggets of gold in this book, I am sure you will find it useful.

Enjoy the story as it takes you on their journey and take the time to reflect on your own circumstances. The more you understand about yourself and others, the stronger your relationships and your successes will become.

Christine

🟢🔴🔵🟡 Christine Kuca-Thompson

🟡🔵🔴🟢 Jennifer Than-Htay

Click! Colours Australia

The Origin and Evolution of the Click! Colours

● ● ● ●

The creators of Click! Colours, Greg Barnes and David Koutsoukis, first met at a National Speakers Association meeting in Perth, Western Australia in 2005. Both accomplished authors, Greg and David swapped books they had written and discovered a common interest in human behaviour and personality tools. They had both been running leadership and team development programs for many years and knew the value of understanding diversity and its many applications. Both had used many different personality models and were accredited in a number of these instruments.

David and Greg became good friends and discussions invariably led to the pros and cons of personality models and other psychometric tools. It was during one of these discussions that they thought, 'Why don't we make our own system that takes the best features of other models and puts them into one package?' Greg then suggested, 'Why don't we create a product and sell it to other facilitators!' David agreed that it was a great idea.

And so, Click! Colours were born. Not long after they were released, and without any promotion or marketing, they found that demand for their new tool was so high that they decided they might need to get serious.

Better, Faster, Cheaper, Easier

At the time of developing the new tool, David was listening to a Brian Tracy audio program. He heard something that captured his attention… 'What businesses want is a "better, faster, cheaper or easier" way of doing things.' This made perfect sense for developing the new tool and addressed some of the key limitations of existing instruments.

With 'Better, Faster, Cheaper and Easier' as their motto, David and Greg started to develop criteria for their new tool. They examined dozens of different personality models (57 to be exact) and picked out what they considered to be the best features of each. Greg had also previously developed a tool called the Genie Cards that became a starting point for the new product.

There's an old saying that goes, 'There's nothing new under the sun; it's all in the way it's spun.' The next section reveals the philosophy behind the development of Click! Colours, and the criteria Greg and David used to spin an old message in a new way to create a better, faster, cheaper and easier personality tool.

WHAT makes the Click! Colours better, faster, cheaper and easier?

The Best of All Worlds

Historically, there have been dozens, if not hundreds of personality concepts, tools and models. The Click! Colours have drawn on the best aspects of these models to create a simple tool that we believe is better, faster, cheaper and easier – and more fun!

The power of the Click! Colours lies in its simplicity. Instead of dozens of questions, computer logins, pre-briefings, debriefings, expensive fees and complicated reports, we have four simple cards. They are effective because they are easy to access, use and understand – and in busy workplaces it's the simple things that work.

Although they are simple, the Click! Colours are powerful. You will see by the development criteria below that the cards have been strategically designed for maximum impact. When you combine this with the unique Click! Colours methodology, you get an enjoyable, memorable and highly effective learning experience.

Delivering an Old Message a New Way

Greg and David created six key criteria they used for the development of the Click! Colours tool and methodology to help deliver an 'old message in a new way'. The Click! Colours were designed to be:

Useful and Useable

The Click! Colours are easy to understand and deliver an affordable, portable and simple process for improving relationships, communication, teamwork, leadership, and decision-making.

Engaging

The Click! Colours are fun, non-threatening, use humour, harness the power of whole-brain thinking and utilise multiple intelligences theory including auditory, visual and kinaesthetic learning styles.

Memorable

The Click! Colours use the four-quadrant format to aid recall and utilises memory hooks, labels, colours, shapes and characters to reinforce and embed learning. Even the Click! Colours name reflects the benefit. That is, Click! Colours help you Click! with people.

Effective

The Click! Colours provide a common language that promotes a shared understanding and has a suite of resources to reinforce key messages. This ensures that the learning continues long after the program has been delivered.

Address the Limitations of Existing Tools

The Click! Colours are a dynamic tool that allows shifting within different contexts. It does not require questionnaires, computer logins, or confusing statistics, and does not label people as one type. It can be facilitated in many ways and is accessible and easy to remember.

Easy to Implement Across Teams and Organisations

The Click! Colours are easy to facilitate. The resources are highly visible and utilise memorable and repeatable bites of learning that are easily shared across teams and organisations.

For more detailed information about the criteria used to develop the Click! Colours, check out the Facilitator Resources section at the end of this book.

●●●● David Koutsoukis

Co-founder of Click! Colours

The Story

This book introduces you to the fascinating story of four colourful characters who work at an organisation called Spectrum Enterprises to demonstrate how and why people behave the way they do...

Spectrum Enterprises is like no other workplace. Despite the diverse array of individuals and personalities, it is the most harmonious, happy and successful organisation ever. The team members at Spectrum are positive, productive and produce exceptional results. Even their home life is almost idyllic.

But it wasn't always that way...

In the early days at Spectrum, conflict was rife. Communication was appalling, teamwork was nonexistent, and meetings would often end in chaos. There was a definite lack of tolerance and understanding among team members. And a lot of issues were flowing over to their friends and families. Comments like 'They just make no sense' were common in the days before the team discovered how to use diversity to their advantage.

So, get ready to experience the journey of discovery we have scoped out for you through the experiences of our colourful characters as they travel 'through the colours of life'. We trust that the pieces of gold you pick up along the way will help you, like them, build fantastic relationships and bring you great success and happiness.

1
Successful People Understand People!

Great relationships are the foundation of all success.

Spectrum Enterprises is like no other workplace. It is the most harmonious, happy and successful organisation you will ever see.

Like any organisation, Spectrum Enterprises is blessed with a diverse array of people. Each person brings to work their own unique personality, experience, beliefs, values and issues. Yet at Spectrum, the air is not full of petty squabbles, ego wrestling or daily frustration at the behaviour of others. At Spectrum, it's as if the 'magic wand' of true teamwork has cast its spell.

The reason Spectrum is so much more successful than any other organisation seems invisible at first. The secrets to such an outstanding culture are not apparent until you 'live' in their workplace for some time.

The first thing you notice is the amount of casual chatter and friendly banter that occurs. You then discover smiling faces everywhere. And lastly, you notice the serious professional respect that is shown when people are solving important problems.

The fundamental difference between Spectrum and most other organisations then becomes apparent.

At Spectrum, it is obvious they have built an environment of tolerance, understanding and trust that goes much further than a plaque on the wall titled Core Values. The people at Spectrum Enterprises really understand each other. They listen to each other and search for meaning in what the other person is saying, rather than judging or simply waiting for a chance to speak themselves. They respect and value diversity as a key ingredient to a successful home and workplace. Differing points of view and ways of seeing the world are sought after, rather than avoided.

So how did the people at Spectrum make this almost ideal workplace happen?

They did it by building a deep understanding of each other. They have developed an understanding of how each person thinks, communicates, problem solves, and why they behave the way they do. They also understand what implications these individual and group differences have on the way they operate and cooperate as one team.

By understanding and respecting the unique attributes, beliefs, personalities, and capabilities of others, they have formed the ideal high-performance team. More importantly, they also understand and leverage their own personal likes and dislikes, as well as the likes and dislikes of others, to build great relationships both at work and at home.

The team members at Spectrum Enterprises have great relationships and produce outstanding results because they recognise that successful people understand people. They have made it 'the way we do things around here' because of the enormous benefits they have gained in all facets of their work and home life.

But it wasn't always that way…

1st Piece of Gold

Understanding people's thinking and behaviour will help you build relationships and achieve success in all aspects of your life.

2
People Are Different!

'Society is like a crowd in carnival costumes.'

Vernon Howard

Here begins our fascinating tale of four very different characters and their journey of discovery as employees of Spectrum Enterprises.

We start at the 'Age of Innocent Ignorance', when everyone lived within their own cocoon, remarkably unaware of how they affected others. They found that they CLICKED with some people straight away, and yet others were incredibly frustrating and the simplest of things annoyed them.

Let's meet our characters.

PEOPLE ARE DIFFERENT!

Yuri sees the world as an exciting place to explore and have fun. He is the ultimate risk-taker. Even his investments are in high growth/high risk shares. Yuri always has at least five projects on the go, most of which he never completes because he often gets distracted and moves onto something new. People often tell him he should be more focussed and should stop interrupting people and completing their sentences for them. He argues that he already knows what they are going to say, and besides, they are taking too long to come to a decision. Yuri's biggest frustration is with people who don't see the 'big picture' and who aren't creative and impulsive like he is. He CLICKS with people who are outgoing and fun but sometimes clashes with those who want to stick to the rules and do things by the book.

Gail's key task each day is to tick off her checklist and tidy her office. She can't understand why the rest of the world (especially Yuri) can't just follow the rules. Her investments are very safe. All her money is in the bank, with any extra being used to pay off her mortgage. Gail sometimes annoys others by 'dotting the i's and crossing the t's' and by writing 7/10 on lengthy reports that only require her signature. 'Someone has to ensure that nothing slips through the cracks,' she argues. But what really makes Gail angry is people (like Yuri) who don't follow procedures – even the ones they have personally agreed to.

Rose really enjoys the company of others, though sometimes feels drained by co-workers who always tell her their problems. They leave her to worry about them all weekend, only to find on Monday they have forgotten all about them! She struggles with her own need to feel empathy for them days after they have moved on. Others notice that she has given names to inanimate objects – her car is called 'Sally', and she affectionately refers to her computer as 'Cal'. Rose often gets told (usually by Bert) that she is too trusting and gullible. This she finds hard to understand since Trust and Respect are two of the core values plastered on most office walls. Not much frustrates or annoys Rose, though she does get somewhat upset when people are dismissive or don't listen to her.

And last but not least, we have Bert, who is constantly frustrated at the lack of logic and rational thought that threatens to ruin his company's bottom line. Without him, this organisation would be broke, he surmises. His investments are thoroughly researched. Although he noticed by the time he finished his two-year analysis of which house to buy, the price had gone up by 45%. Bert's favourite hobby is playing chess. Oddly enough, some colleagues have told him they feel uncomfortable discussing issues with

him as they feel as though he is playing chess with their minds. He dismisses such comments as the failings of people who are not his intellectual equal – such as Gail and Yuri, or worse, illogical people like Rose. The best way to annoy Bert is to turn up at his office with a half-baked idea that has not been researched and has no supporting business plan.

Amazingly, all four of our characters work in the same organisation. This is amazing because all four would tell you that they would be very unlikely to mix with the others outside of work. They live in very different suburbs, and they all enjoy very different holidays. Yuri enjoys white-water rafting and parachuting, while Bert likes to visit science exhibitions and attend his debating club. Gail prefers staying home and gardening, and Rose loves visiting friends and relatives.

As you can imagine, the interaction among these four quite different people has not always been positive. In fact, the one thing they do have in common is that at some time they have all privately thought or exclaimed to themselves, 'Why do I CLICK with some people and CLASH with others?!'

2nd Piece of Gold

People are different, and this diversity impacts on all aspects of life.

3

Diversity Impacts on the Workplace

'You must look into people, as well as at them.'

Lord Chesterfield

Meetings can be the bane of an employee's day, and at Spectrum Enterprises, today is no different.

Bert (Finance Manager of 15 years), Rose (HR Manager for 4 years), Yuri (Marketing Manager since moving from Sales last year), and Gail (Safety and Quality Control Manager since the company was established 28 years ago) are about to attend a meeting called by Gail to organise this year's strategic planning process.

Yuri actually enjoys meetings as long as there is plenty of brainstorming and sharing of creative ideas (preferably his own). His only concern about meetings is that sometimes he looks around and notices that no-one is listening to him or taking him seriously. He finds this very strange since he regards himself as highly creative, a visionary and very clever. In fact, to the best of his knowledge, he has never been wrong about anything.

Rose loves meetings as they provide a chance for people interaction, albeit in a more sterile environment than she would like. So long as there is no conflict at the meeting, and as long as she doesn't have to voice her opinion before she feels comfortable to do so, the gathering of people around a table is potentially one of the highlights of her day. Meetings would almost be nirvana if they could just spend most of the time discussing people, relationships and teamwork issues in an open, friendly environment.

Bert can't understand why they have to have meetings at all, especially when they are going to discuss Strategic Business Issues. Surely it makes more sense to simply ask his team to build the business models required and present them together, with the appropriate spreadsheets, at the normal weekly management meeting. The only possible upside to having a meeting would be if they allowed him to present his slides to the entire Senior Management group so he could finally convince them about the value of downsizing. Still, if they really want to have such silly meetings, he better attend so his boss doesn't comment about him not being a team player again (whatever that meant).

Gail insists that this meeting is essential. She argues it is needed to plan and organise the details of the Strategic Planning Process. They need to determine what the logistical requirements are, decide who will coordinate the process and determine how they will make sure that everything sticks to schedule and proceed according to plan (unlike last year). Besides, Gail considers that meetings can be very productive if participants just stick to the agenda and timings.

Gail arrives at meeting room 717A fifteen minutes early with her agenda and last year's follow-up action plan neatly organised in her Strategic Planning Process folder.

Bert is next to arrive with his personal computer complete with next year's forecasts and business model already loaded.

Rose is five minutes late, and she apologises profusely, explaining that she would have been on time, but someone stopped her in the passageway with a staff problem that couldn't wait.

They all wait for Yuri, who strolls in 20 minutes late, stands next to the flip chart and proceeds to draw a Genie coming out of a bottle under which he writes, 'Brainstorming Topic = What is our Genie Vision for this Company?'

Bert immediately folds his arms. Gail sighs and closes her folder over her carefully compiled agenda. And Rose starts to fret because this meeting looks like going the way of so many others.

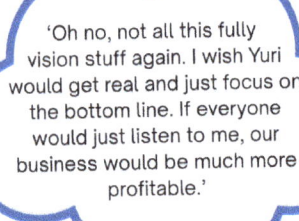

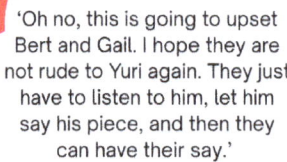

Yuri turns to see Bert with his arms folded, sitting back in his chair, frowning. Gail is looking down at the agenda, and Rose has what he suspects is a sympathetic look on her face – but he couldn't be sure as people have told him that he is not very good at recognising subtle signals. But Yuri can spot the super obvious signs that – apart from Rose – no one is listening to him.

Gail spoke next. 'I think we should start at Item #1 on the agenda entitled Planning Workshop Logistics. We can leave the 'vision' segment until we hold the workshop.'

'Sounds logical to me,' says Bert. 'But I don't understand why we need to have this workshop in the first place. Why can't we just use the models my Finance Department has built from our existing data and analysis?'

'Because we need some vision. We need to explore the big picture. Think outside the box. Challenge paradigms and seek high-performance breakthroughs,' interrupted Yuri. 'That's what I have been saying all along, but you lot don't seem to listen. We need to be more aspirational, go for exponential growth and adopt best practice,' he continued.

'Please, let's listen to Gail,' said the softly spoken Rose. 'She has the role of organising this workshop so let's give her some help.'

'Good, thanks Rose – now let's start with Item #1, which is deciding where we will hold this two-day Strategic Planning Workshop,' said Gail, with some relief evident in her voice.

And so the meeting progressed, with varying levels of frustration. The only outcome, after running 30 minutes late, was that all agreed that Gail should research venues, seek an experienced external facilitator and send out invitations.

Bert left, vowing to never attend another fluffy meeting again. People who didn't focus on facts and arrive at logical conclusions frustrate him. He couldn't understand wasting so much time without any bottom-line results.

Yuri was excited, as usual, if only because they were going to have a workshop. He thought it might be fun, even though last year's was almost a disaster.

Gail was upset that she had to do all the work again, though she secretly admitted to herself that at least if she did it, it would be done right.

And Rose felt sorry for the others. She was mildly upset with the lack of listening and lack of seeking to understand each other's point of view. Plus, no-one asked her for her opinion or thoughts.

3rd Piece of Gold

Personality styles impact on how people think, feel and act at work.

4

Diversity Impacts on the Home

'If we are to live together in peace, we must come to know each other better.'

Lyndon B. Johnson

'Another day – another dollar,' thought Bert as he drove his car out of his private car space marked Finance Manager Only. He had achieved some things today, despite that dreadful meeting.

He thought the Performance Appraisal he conducted with one of his team went well, though he was still at a loss to understand why she left his office crying. After all, he only told her the truth about how she could lift her performance above the B+ he had awarded her. Didn't she understand that he almost never gave an 'A' to anyone, no matter how good they were? Perhaps he should read that book Rose had given him. What was it called again? Something about the importance of people or was it about coaching and mentoring?

Never mind, at least the monthly figures looked good when he e-mailed them to his boss, the Finance Director, before leaving the office. Now he was keen to get to his home office where he could work in peace and quiet on his analysis of cost drivers that affect the business. Away from continual interruptions from his staff and people from other departments, and away from those silly questions they should have thought through themselves before bothering him.

'Don't come to me with your problems – come with rational solutions,' he would constantly urge, wondering 'What is wrong with them? Can't they think for themselves?'

'Oh well, soon I will be in the solitude of my other office,' he thought, as he drove towards his house.

'I just hope my daughter doesn't want to play as soon as I get home. I'll have to tell my wife to instruct her again that 6-7.30 pm is my home office slot, and I will help her with homework after dinner… if I have time,' he reminded himself.

But when Bert got home, little Yasmin was already waiting for him on her bike in the carport.

'Hi Daddy! Let's go to the park and play on the swings!' she called, as he got his briefcase out of the car.

'Not now, Yasmin. Wait until I have finished my work. Maybe after dinner. Besides, have you finished your homework yet?' he said, striding away.

'Doesn't Daddy realise that it will be dark after dinner and time for me to go to bed again like last time?' thought Yasmin, as she hopped off her bike and walked despondently across to the park by herself. It really annoyed her that Daddy's work always seemed to be more important than she was.

'What is wrong with him?' she wondered. 'Is his work really more important than I am?'

Inside, Bert's wife Rita was in her studio painting. She wasn't the greatest artist in the world and frankly, she didn't aspire to be. Despite Bert's continued suggestions that she should take lessons so she could sell some art, she more enjoyed the meditative effects of painting.

'What would you like for dinner?' she asked, while trying to catch up to him for a welcome home kiss on the way to his home office.

'Oh, anything will do,' he replied, wondering why she even asked him in the first place. Couldn't she see that he had his mind on far more important things? He was impatient to review the economic modelling he had done on a possible cost-cutting program he was keen to implement back at work. He had already identified a 20% cost saving if he could convince the boss to sack the 30 people he had identified as either redundant (in his mind), or who could be outsourced. For instance, what bottom line value do we get from Human Resources and Training Departments he asked himself? Yet, whenever he presented his ideas, no-one seemed to listen. But if he could build a compelling business case, then they would have to listen to him.

Downstairs, Rita walked towards the kitchen shaking her head. 'Why can't Bert see that he should be playing more with Yasmin?' she thought. 'Every time I try to discuss Yasmin or even talk about our relationship he doesn't seem to listen. And when I finally corner him with such issues (usually when we are on vacation), he either gets upset and accuses me of trying to ruin our holiday, or gets ultra-defensive as though I am attacking him. Or worse, he goes into problem-solving mode and keeps offering solutions or corrective strategies, as he calls them. Give me a break!'

Inside his own head, Bert was totally oblivious to what was happening at home. In his mind, life was normal; sometimes okay, sometimes not. Yet he often suspected that something was missing in his life. Real happiness somehow seemed to elude him. And his constant analysing of his family and home situation had yet to uncover what the problem was – let alone any possible solutions.

So, Bert continued the same 'self-talk' whose rationale had maintained him over the years.

Rose left the office not long after Bert. She would have left earlier to be home with her family by 5pm if one of Bert's team hadn't approached her in the canteen with tears in her eyes. She had been crying on and off for most of the afternoon, devastated by the constructive criticism that Bert had given her.

'I thought I had done a great job all year,' she blurted to Rose. 'He even awarded me a B+ which, while not as high as my previous boss's A's, still had me pretty happy. But then he spent the whole performance appraisal telling me how I could improve. Not one word about what I was doing well. And when I pressed him for specific examples of where I had displeased him, he came up with some petty graphs I had produced for one of his presentations months ago. Why didn't he just tell me at the time and I could have changed them?' she sobbed.

Rose was still worrying about how she could help her build a better relationship with Bert when she drove into her garage. Even as she walked to her backyard to find her children, she started to dread the inevitable conflict that would happen when she finally got up the courage to have another discussion with Bert about how to treat people properly.

'Our organisation is all about people, not numbers. In fact, I wish I could call my department the People Department instead of Human Resources,' she would repeat, expecting the same blank look she got from most people at work who experienced this diatribe.

But at least Rose was home now, she thought, and the feeling of belonging returned to her heart. The warm glow of being home increased when she spotted her children, Robbie and Gretel, playing on the swing.

'Can I push you guys?' she enquired.

'Yeah, that would be great, Mum,' they responded, and suddenly life was good again for Rose.

Rose found her mind drifting as she gently pushed the swings and smiled at her children.

'I wonder why home life is so peaceful – almost meditative for me – yet work is so full of stress?' she pondered.

'I know I shouldn't be judgmental, but perhaps there is something wrong with a lot of those people at work. Maybe I am missing something? I try to understand them. I certainly listen to all their issues, problems and concerns. I give them the benefit of the doubt when they say or do something that upsets me or others. Yet things aren't getting any better. They continue to surprise me with their selfish behaviour, rude interruptions, silly rules, and lack of respect for others, no matter how much they claim to be team players. Perhaps I should find another workplace. One where adults act like adults – respect each other and don't behave like spoilt children,' she thought.

'Mummy, are you okay?' asked Robbie in a tone which weirdly reminded Rose so much of herself.

'Yes, I'm fine – now,' Rose replied. 'Let's take your sister inside and read her a book before dinner,' she said.

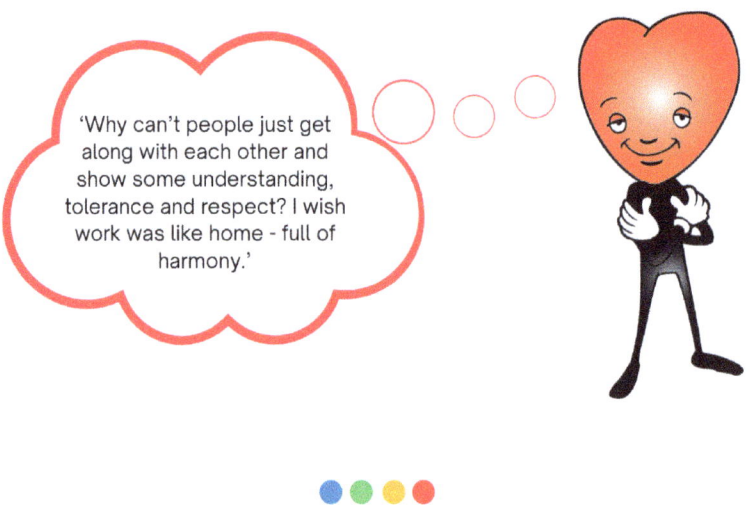

Yuri also left the office later than expected, but it was because he was having so much fun at work.

He had pushed aside everything else on his desk to draw up the grand 'Genie Vision' he had started during the ill-fated meeting. He was so excited about creating a new organisation that he took the flip chart from the meeting room back to his office, grabbed some multi-coloured pens and started drawing his vision.

Occasionally, Yuri did reflect that perhaps this vision was a bit extreme for a company of only 60 people. But he stopped himself from thinking small by reminding himself, to be truly great, you need to have outlandish ambitions (or something like that he heard from one of the numerous motivational speakers he listened to and had forgotten over the years).

When he did finally arrive home, Yuri burst into his house and startled his family (as he was inclined to do). They were about to sit down for dinner, but he suggested they all jump in the pool and play with him before dinner.

'Come on, honey, come on, kids, let's have some fun on such a lovely evening!' he exclaimed.

'Okay, Dad!' his little girl responded, but his son stared at him in disbelief while his wife put her head in her hands in desperation.

'Yuri, it's dinnertime! You know we always have dinner at this time,' she said. 'Besides, the pool is freezing this time of year, and the children have just had their baths!'

'Oh, okay then,' he surrendered and went off to change into something more comfortable.

Yanie, his eight-year-old, was disappointed that Mum had spoiled the fun again, while Garry, his six-year-old, smiled because now he didn't have to climb into that cold pool and could eat his dinner instead.

Yuri was not upset with his wife for spoiling his fun – again. He was not the sort of person to hold grudges. Besides, he believed in moving on and letting little things like that pass over him 'like water off a duck's back'. But he did wonder why his wife and son didn't get more excited about life.

'They just don't seem to get it,' he thought to himself as he changed out of his work clothes.

Most of his grand ideas at home seemed to get a similar treatment to those at work. Some people, like his daughter did get it. She seemed to CLICK into his wavelength and instantly join his enthusiasm. While others would annoy him by being 'old stick-in-the-muds', not wanting to 'rock the boat'.

'Why isn't everyone like me?' he mused, as he checked his reflection in the bathroom mirror. 'Surely life is for living, and that means taking risks and being impulsive sometimes.'

Still, he conformed, once again, and sat down with his family for an orderly dinner. But, as usual, the chatter in his mind would not stop, so he heard little of the conversation that took place around the table.

DIVERSITY IMPACTS ON THE HOME

Gail mused on the way home about why she always seemed to be the last to leave the office. 'I can't understand it. I am the most organised person I know, yet I never leave at 5pm like it says in my daily diary.'

For a person who is never late for any appointment (in fact, she is even *early* for doctor's appointments – despite knowing that the doctor will always be running behind schedule), leaving this late from the office was a bigger issue than it was for Yuri, Rose or Bert.

'Never mind,' she thought. 'I'll just have to do another check of my list of tasks and work out where my schedule is upset. At least everything I had on my checklist for today has been ticked off and completed, which is more than I can say for the rest of my team.'

Being in control and in her comfort zone was especially important for Gail.

It was because of this that her mood changed as soon as she saw that her 20-year-old son had parked his car in her spot again!

'Bodhi!' she yelled as she hopped out of her car. 'Move your car out of my spot. I want to sweep the garage and wash my car before dinner!'

Bodhi didn't hear her as the music in his room was too loud, and besides, he and his girlfriend were trying out his latest toy – new state-of-the-art headphones.

'Never mind, I'll do it myself – again,' she decided, and went searching for his car keys. Eventually, after:

1. Finding Bodhi's car keys,

2. Moving her car so she could move his,

3. Moving his car,

4. Sweeping clean her spot in the garage where his car had been,

5. Moving her car into 'her spot',

6. Washing and drying her car,

7. Finding her husband down in the tool shed and reminding him it was his turn to cook dinner,

8. Getting changed out of her work clothes and putting out the next day's clothes ready for the morning,

9. Replacing the toilet paper roll that her husband had put on the 'wrong way' again,

10. Setting the table after making sure her husband had dinner under control,

11. And dragging Bodhi and his girlfriend out of his room for dinner…

… she could finally sit down and have dinner.

A pleasant experience for her, but not so for the others, as they had to sit through a long and detailed description of how hard her day was. Particularly disastrous was the meeting to organise the Strategic Planning Workshop. They heard all about her frustrations with people who couldn't stick to agendas and who didn't understand the importance of getting every detail right so nothing can go wrong.

'They are so frustrating!' she exclaimed. 'How could anyone be so careless as to risk booking a venue without the proper amenities in each room?' she said.

Bodhi didn't mind this ongoing outburst as much as his dad. He had decided to wear his new headphones so he could only hear bits of what his mum was saying during breaks in the music.

Yanos, her husband, was less fortunate. He desperately wanted the attention to turn to him so he could tell everyone about the new invention he was building down in the shed. But no matter how many times he tried to share his excitement with his family, no-one seemed interested. And besides, he couldn't get a word in anyway!

Later that night, after carefully stacking the dishwasher, Gail reflected on her day as she lay in bed.

Again and again, the people in her life seemed to frustrate her at every turn. People would turn up late for meetings at work. Others would arrive unprepared – some even forgot the agenda she had sent them days before. And what really frustrated her were those people who would get so distracted by other issues that only the first couple of items on the agenda got discussed before they had to rush off to another meeting.

Then, at home, her husband and son acted like they were aliens. They never tidied up their stuff and seemed oblivious to her house schedule. How many times did she have to remind them that dinner was at 6pm and bedtime was at 9pm? They didn't even know how to fold towels correctly, for goodness' sake!

'Don't people understand that there are rules? Am I the only one who cares about being on time and organised? And why do things have to keep on changing? If it ain't broke, don't fix it! I wish life was more stable and less chaotic.'

4th Piece of Gold

Personality impacts how people think, feel and act at home.

5

Great Relationships and Teamwork Don't 'Just Happen'

Relationships are built on understanding. Understanding requires knowledge.

Leaving her house early, on the way to the workshop she had organised, Gail was fretting, despite the fact that she had double-checked every item on her checklist. She even ticked off the type, number and colour of flip chart pens requested by the facilitator they hired. Just why the facilitator needed 4 x blue, 4 x red, 4 x yellow and 4 x green pens was beyond her.

'Now it's just up to everyone else to make this workshop a success after all the hard work I have put into it,' she thought as she slowed, approaching some traffic lights.

GREAT RELATIONSHIPS AND TEAMWORK DON'T 'JUST HAPPEN' 47

This thought, however, sent a shiver down her spine as she remembered last year's workshop and how Yuri and Bert had behaved.

A calming influence returned when she remembered the amount of detailed preparation she had put into the logistics, and the meticulous care she and Rose had taken to choose a professional facilitator this year. They briefed the facilitator in depth to avoid a repeat of last year's debacle, and they stressed that great relationships and teamwork were just as important to them as the Strategic Plan output.

'We can always write up the Strategic Plan back at work,' they had explained to the facilitator. 'But we will never be able to get buy-in and ownership unless we all work as a team to build it.'

Despite the successful facilitator briefing, Gail was still worried about the facilitator. How would they cope with the strength of Yuri and especially Bert's characters?

Her confidence lifted as Gail remembered the impeccable track record the facilitator had with some of the world's top companies. If she can keep those folks in order, she thought, then surely, she could handle the likes of Yuri and Bert. But the experience of last year's workshop, which she had tried to facilitate herself, left her with a feeling of dread. Gail just couldn't see how anyone could get them all to agree. Yes, Rose would cooperate, but how is anyone, no matter how good, going to get Bert and Yuri to see eye to eye?

When the others arrived, the conference room was like nothing they had seen before, and all the usual judgmental thoughts emerged.

'Not another fluffy waste of time,' thought Bert. 'I knew this was a mistake. If the facilitator tries to get us to do any group hugs, I'm out of here!'

'How could any supposed professional put up a wallchart so crooked?' was Gail's first impression.

'Oh no! This type of room set-up will antagonise Bert,' Rose worried, as she walked over to greet the facilitator.

Interestingly, the 'quirkiness' of the room set-up – with chairs in a circle, multi-coloured wall charts and post-it notes on the floor (because all the tables had been removed) – elicited a very different reaction from Yuri. 'This could be fun,' he thought with a smile.

Gail, however, was still wearing a worried face, which deepened when the facilitator (who was dressed casually in multi coloured clothes) began by placing a bell and rainbow coloured timer on the floor next to her stool whilst chatting to Rose, who was listening intently to every word.

'Great, now that everyone is here, let's get started on-time for a change,' remarked Gail.

'Excellent,' said the facilitator, as they all took their seats.

'This workshop will be like no other you have ever attended,' the facilitator announced to the dismay of Bert, who was already leaning back in his chair with his arms folded.

'My name is Leica Rainbow, and in 20 years of facilitating workshops, I have learnt that unless you build a team of focused, aligned, passionate and committed people, then a strategic plan is not worth the paper it is written on,' she stated, as she flashed her first slide on the conference room screen.

> Nobody has it ALL together
> but
> TOGETHER we have it ALL!

'Just a little thought provoker to stimulate our thinking,' she continued.

Bert glanced fiercely at Gail, who was desperately trying to avoid his gaze. 'You are about to experience something very special as I coach you all through a journey of self-discovery,' said the almost hypnotic facilitator. 'You see, Strategic Plans are but mere wads of paper. Far more important to any organisation or culture are the people, relationships and teams who contribute to their success. So rather than starting with traditional planning processes, I am going to start with a team and relationship-building exercise I call:

Living in a Rainbow

Through it, we will discover 'Who **you** are, who **they** are, and why people behave differently'. This exercise will rapidly bond us as a team and set the foundation for how we will work together. It will expose the spectrum of diversity that exists, even in our small group. Additionally, the knowledge and tools you will learn will help you build quality relationships, success and happiness at both work and home.'

5th Piece of Gold

We can boost relationships by understanding why people behave the way they do (including ourselves!).

Checkpoint 1

Checkpoints have been included to help you get the most out of this book. Their purpose is to get you to pause, reflect and consider the information you have taken in so far.

Recognising Behaviour Patterns

By now you will have noticed that our four characters have demonstrated certain personality traits.

1. What behaviours do you recognise in yourself?

_____

_____

_____

2. What behaviours do you recognise in colleagues?

_____

_____

_____

3. What behaviours do you recognise in family members?

_____

_____

_____

4. Have you been annoyed at, or judgmental of, any of these behaviours recently?

_____

_____

_____

The next few chapters will explain the behaviour of our four characters and demonstrate how to identify them in your colleagues, customers, families, friends and, of course, in ourselves.

Once we have identified these patterns of behaviour, we can use this knowledge in all facets of life so that 'living with people' becomes a more joyful experience, rather than a constantly challenging and occasionally frustrating one.

6

Everyone Has Four Sub-Personalities

'Seek first to understand, then be understood.'

Stephen Covey

Leica Rainbow had conducted her "Living in a Rainbow" exercise many times, yet it still intrigued her to see the reactions of participants. One thing she discovered was common to all people – they all loved to learn about themselves.

'Let's start the activity,' said Leica. 'It's an interactive exercise that explores individual and group diversity.'

'No group hugs, I hope!' interrupted Bert.

'You're safe, Bert, no hugs … for now,' she replied with an endearing smile.

'This simple yet powerful exercise has three key steps, which we will walk through together on our journey of discovery,' she continued as she flashed a slide outlining the steps.

> **Step 1. Understand Yourself**
>
> (Who am I - really?
> And why do I behave the way I do?)
>
> **Step 2. Understand Others**
>
> (Who are they - really?
> And why do they behave the way they do?)
>
> **Step 3. Understand the Implications**
>
> (How can understanding each other help us in our relationships, teamwork and life in general?

'So, let's start our journey to what I call the Pot of Gold at the End of the Rainbow,' Leica stated, now that she had their undivided attention. 'We'll start the same way you would on any journey – with the first step.'

> ## Step 1. Understand Yourself
> Who am I - really?
> And why do I behave the way I do?

'First, you must understand yourself,' said Leica. 'So, to truly help you understand yourselves I am going to give each of you four cards I call "Click! Colour Cards" – a Red Carer card, a Green Safekeeper card, a Yellow Playmaker card, and a Blue Analyser card. Together, these four cards represent the four key sub-personalities that combine to make a whole person.

'Exploring these four coloured cards is like discovering your own Personal Rainbow,' she continued. 'Each of us has all of these colours, but some colours shine brighter than others!' she concluded.

'Your task is to read each card with what I call a "child's mindset". Be playful, act naïvely and have an open mind, like a young child. Don't be judgmental. Don't take yourself too seriously. Don't dismiss these cards simply because they appear too simplistic – as adults tend to do. And above all, make sure you have fun with this activity!' she said.

Bert couldn't believe what was happening. 'This is absurd! How can four silly coloured cards help me understand myself? She has already said I am complex, so where is the complex analytical model I can use to compute my personality?' Bert dismissed the cards as a childish game, despite the advice Leica had given.

Yuri, on the other hand, thought this was great fun, as he read the Yellow Playmaker card (but forgot to read the other cards as instructed).

Gail was almost as flustered as Bert, but for a different reason. She was worried that she might miss something important in the cards that could cause her to make a mistake.

Rose was the calmest of all. Like Yuri, she found it quite easy to relate back to her childhood – acting naïvely and keeping an open mind. Besides, everything she read on the cards not only reminded her of parts of herself, but also of other people she knew.

'Now that you have read the Click! Colour Cards, put them in order – like a stack of playing cards – with the card that you believe is "most like you" on top of the pile, then the card which is next most "like you", then "somewhat like you" and on the bottom place the card which is "least like you",' Leica instructed.

'Now, remember that each of us has all four of these cards within us, but we all have preferences – no matter how slight – that allow us to rank these cards from "most like me" to "least like me",' she stated, knowing that some cards would appeal more to some of them than others.

Yuri looked at the cards and immediately picked the Yellow card with a smile on his face. He didn't even look at the other cards as he waited impatiently for the others to finish making their choices.

Gail was frustrated as she tried to put all four cards in order from the one that was most like her, down to the card she felt was least like her. Not an easy task when your primary concern is to not make a mistake.

Bert was reading the cards intensely and decided:

1. He was all of these cards and no clear preference should or could emerge.

2. It was wrong to choose one without proper analysis. Besides, even when these silly games are played with more qualitative diagnostic tools like questionnaires, they are still full of generalisations and tend to stereotype people. In any case, who cares what personalities we have so long as we get the job done, he thought, and then proceeded to analyse the other people in the room.

Rose's first response was not even directed at the cards in her hands. Rather, her first concern was that this revealing of one's true self may be embarrassing for some people. She hoped that no one would be put on the spot or get too defensive about sharing personal information.

Then, after what Gail and Bert thought was far too short a period to get it right, Leica rang her bell.

'As you came in this morning, you would have noticed the coloured wall charts in each corner of the room,' she stated, as she pointed to each one.

'I would now like you to take your four cards and go stand next to the coloured wall chart which you believe is most like you,' she instructed.

Yuri immediately strode towards the Yellow Wall Chart with Leica close behind, carrying his other three cards, which he had absent-mindedly left behind.

Gail went over to the Green Wall Chart and started to straighten it, while Rose stood quietly at the Red Wall Chart, feeling a little lonely and exposed.

Meanwhile, Leica was counselling Bert that, 'Yes, you are all four cards, but would you like to stand next to the Blue Wall Chart for now? You can do a more in-depth analysis later.'

Once they were in their corners, Leica asked each of them to explain why they had chosen that particular colour card as being 'most like them'.

Yuri immediately responded in a rapid-fire excited voice, 'Because I like taking risks, being impulsive and having grand schemes.'

He then proceeded to list the many outrageous things he had done in his life, such as buying cars and even a house on impulse. And how he would often suffer buyer's remorse when he realised he had not analysed the market, checked his list of requirements or even consulted his family before making the purchase.

Gail joined in explaining how she felt like tidying up other people's desks and filing systems at work. And how even at home she folded towels and socks a certain way and straightened pictures on the wall. She was also proud of the fact that her money was safe and secure in the bank and not being risked in stocks or other investments. And she would never buy anything that didn't match her checklist!

Bert said he wanted more time to consider why this might be his preferred card among the four choices he was given. He asked if he could take the cards away and do some in-depth analysis for discussion at a later date, so Leica allowed him some thinking time and moved on to Rose.

Rose had a revelation. 'I think I now know why people at work often approach me with their problems even when I hardly know them. Like this Red card says – people must sense that I will listen to them and provide a sympathetic ear,' she surmised. 'I often find out that they had previously talked to others, but felt that they either didn't seem to care or in some cases even seemed glad that someone else had problems. Also, I often find myself crying at movies, then looking around to see others simply watching the screen impassively,' she shared.

Moving back to Bert, Leica managed to get him to admit that he was probably standing against the Blue Chart because he tended to analyse everything.

'My family sometimes think I'm silly because I even analyse going on holiday and am constantly trying to solve their problems rather than just listening to them,' he finally surrendered.

'Good comment, Bert,' Leica responded, 'because it's important that we do not try to analyse every step as we progress through this exercise. Remember, I suggested earlier that we adopt the same mindset we had when we were children learning to walk and talk – be open-minded, be willing to make mistakes, take risks, and have fun learning,' Leica reminded them. 'For if you do keep an open mind, you can learn almost anything!' she concluded, as another slide flashed on the screen.

> Learning about yourself and others is so powerful, it is like finding a **pot of gold** at the end of the rainbow!

As the team members discussed the 'pot of gold', Leica reflected upon where each person in her group would place themselves within a Click! Colours Sub-Personalities Summary.

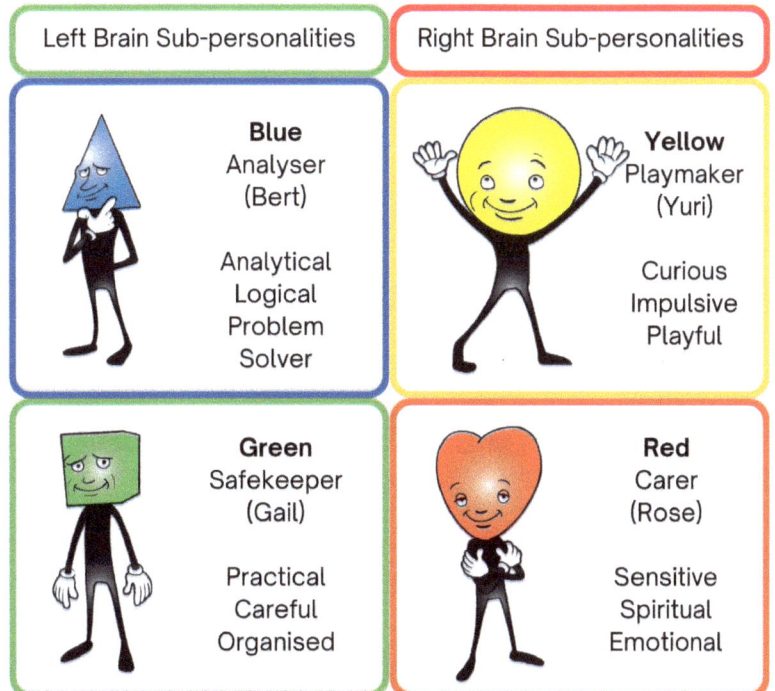

6th Piece of Gold

Our thinking and behaviour are influenced by our four key sub-personalities.

Click! Colours Sub-Personalities Summary

The Analyser
Our analytical, logical and problem-solving side - the Blue band in our rainbow

The Safekeeper
Our practical, careful and organised side - the Green band

The Playmaker
Our curious, impulsive and playful side - the Yellow band

The Carer
Our sensitive, spiritual and emotional side - the Red band

Checkpoint 2

Colourful Characters – Just Like All of Us

By now you may have noticed that our four main characters are very different and unique in their own special way. That's because each represents one of the four sub-personalities that form every person. Some of these sub-personalities dominate our behaviour, while others seem hidden deep down in the recesses of our brain. But whoever we are – they ALL live somewhere within us – and all around us in our family, friends, colleagues, clients, bosses, children, adults, and even strangers we meet.

So, as you read on, relax, smile and appreciate the behaviours, words and thoughts of our four key characters, as you relate to them either personally or through others you know. Vive la différence!

Are you like – or do you know someone like:

Yuri – The Playmaker – Our adventurous, impulsive side. Always seeking fun. Easily bored and distracted. Yuri is represented by the circle icon because Playmakers often get distracted and go off on tangents. They are prone to running around in circles. The bright yellow colour represents their sunny, optimistic disposition.

Bert – The Analyser – Our logical, analytical persona. Constantly seeking rational answers to all problems. Bert is represented by the triangle icon because Analysers can be perceived as sharp thinkers who like to get to the point. The deep blue colour represents their depth of thought and perceived cool demeanour.

Rose – The Carer – Our emotional, spiritual, caring side. In tune with others and nature. Rose is represented by the heart icon since, by nature, Carers tend to have more empathy for others and really care about the wellbeing of people. The red colour represents their warmth and heart-felt aura.

Gail – The Safekeeper – Our practical, organised, risk-averse side. Forever striving to keep the world in order and under control. Gail is represented by the square icon because Safekeepers can be perceived by others as 'square', as they don't like to break rules or take risks. The square also indicates symmetry, organisation and orderliness. The green colour represents their natural, practical outlook.

Character Indicators: Names and Colours

You may have noticed by now that the first letter in our character's names corresponds with the first letter of their dominant sub-personality colour.

For example, **Y**uri = **Y**ellow, **B**ert = **B**lue, **R**ose = **R**ed and **G**ail = **G**reen. You will also find that their family, friends and colleagues follow the same pattern.

Track the behaviours of the characters in the book and enjoy identifying who they remind you of – including yourself!

Gender Differences

Finally, please note that while Yuri, Bert, Rose, and Gail are presented with specific genders in our story, the traits they portray can be expressed by people of any gender or identity. You will discover this fact when you meet their children, spouses, friends and workmates.

7
Some Sub-Personalities 'Shine' Brighter than Others

No two rainbows are identical, but everyone is beautiful!

As each person stood next to his or her 'most preferred' wall chart, Leica pondered how different each of them was.

'Now that you have identified which colour card is most like you, let's explore the rest of the rainbow which makes us a whole person,' Leica suggested. 'Although your top colour may shine brightest, the other colours in your Rainbow also impact on your behaviour, relationships and life choices.'

'So, now I would like you to move to the wall chart that matches the card you believe is "next most like you",' Leica instructed. 'Which colour shines next brightest?' she added as Yuri and Rose smiled.

Rose and Yuri quickly moved to stand next to different wall charts, but Gail, and even more so Bert, hesitated until Leica helped them by saying, 'Remember it's okay to make a mistake. We are simply exploring the Rainbow. This is just an initial exploratory exercise using simple playing cards. You can shuffle and change your choices later if you wish.'

She knew that Bert and Gail would find it hard to make fast intuitive choices. They were being forced out of their comfort zones. Their natural tendency has always been to take time to analyse (Bert), and be careful and safe (Gail).

'Great, now you are at your second-choice colour chart. Most of you should feel pretty comfortable with what is described on this colour card. Not quite as comfortable as with your first choice, but most of the things on the card would still represent how you behave in a neutral environment with few external forces acting to influence unusual behaviour,' Leica said.

'Let's now take another step through the rainbow and move to your third choice. This time to the wall chart that represents the colour card, which is less like you than the first two. Many descriptors on this card may resemble you, but a few more items are popping up which don't seem to fit with how you would normally describe yourself,' Leica added to help them choose their third colour preference.

'Last, but certainly not least, I would now like you to walk to the wall chart, which is least like you. And as you walk there, think about this colour card as it is possibly the most important of all four cards,' Leica remarked.

As soon as they got to their respective corners, Gail asked, 'Why did you say this is possibly the most important card?'

Bert surprised the group by responding immediately to Gail's question. 'I was thinking about that as we walked to our corner as you suggested,' he began.

'Logically, this card is most important because it is our biggest weakness,' Bert stated confidently.

'I'm not sure I would term it a weakness,' replied Rose. 'Maybe this card just suggests some things which we are not necessarily comfortable with or even avoid doing. Like you, Bert. You are standing in the Red corner, suggesting that you may find it harder than me to show and accept emotions. This may make it difficult for you to CLICK with others who are trying to connect with you on an emotional level.'

'Yes, and I find it hard to take risks or accept radical change,' confessed Gail, 'which is why I am standing next to this Yellow chart. I also had to smile as I watched Yuri walk to the Green chart as I often see how impatient he gets when we want more details about some of his grand schemes.'

'I was smiling too,' admitted Yuri. 'As I walked over here, I realised how much I tend to avoid what I would call getting bogged down in detail, yet often those very details end up being so important to the success of my lofty goals.'

'Very good,' replied Leica. 'We are all realising that many things on this "least preferred card" represent thoughts, feelings, beliefs, and behaviours which we are either uncomfortable with, or even try to avoid because they are "just not us". Therefore, this colour card contains – for most of us – our greatest limitations, which when understood and worked on could provide enormous personal growth,' she suggested as her next side appeared.

> The colour that shines least in our 'Rainbow' often reflects our latent power.

'Our greatest potential for growth often lies in this hidden part of us,' Leica continued.

'Yeah, but who says I need to change?' challenged Bert. 'After all, I have been successful, I think, by doing what I've always done. And just because I sometimes annoy or frustrate others doesn't necessarily mean they're right,' Bert concluded.

'Yes, I know what you mean,' Leica said. 'People often do or suggest things that I think are either unfair, untrue, or simply not right. But what I see as their failings may simply be their way of seeing the world. And perhaps, just occasionally, they might actually be right!' she continued.

'Let's try something,' Leica suggested. 'Could everyone please put your hand on your heart and say after me, "I'm okay" – now point to everyone else and say: "It's just all of you who have problems!"' They all laughed as Leica flashed their words up on the screen.

SOME SUB-PERSONALITIES 'SHINE' BRIGHTER THAN OTHERS

> **I'm OK.**
> **It's just all of you who have problems!**

'You see, we can only see the world through our own eyes. That's only natural. But it means that we miss out on seeing the whole rainbow of viewpoints, opinions, out-of-the-box ideas and ways of doing things that are different from our own,' Leica said.

'We all live in our own personal cocoon,' she continued. 'It's safe, comfortable and, most of the time, seems to work for us. However, we sense that life could be so much more fulfilling if only others would play the game of life the way we see it. But how?'

'And that's where Step 2 of the "Living in a Rainbow" exercise comes in. Step 1 was about understanding yourself and recognising why you behave the way you do. Step 2 is about understanding others, and appreciating why they often appear to behave so strangely to us,' she instructed.

'But before we go to Step 2, let's complete what I call the Click Colour Spectrum to summarise what your own, unique, personal Rainbow looks like,' she recommended.

'Sounds like fun! How do we create our own rainbows?' Yuri asked.

'It's easy. All you have to do is colour in the four bands of the Rainbow with the colour that is most like you at the top, down to the colour that is least like you at the bottom. This will give you a graphic representation of your personality,' she instructed. 'Some people even stick their Click Colour Spectrum up at their workstations so that their colleagues will know what makes them tick.'

Checkpoint 3

CLICK! COLOUR SPECTRUM

Colour in your own Click! Colour Spectrum

Colour the top band with your most dominant colour, followed by colouring in the second band with your second colour, the third band with your third colour, and the fourth or smallest band with the colour that is least like you.

Name: _____

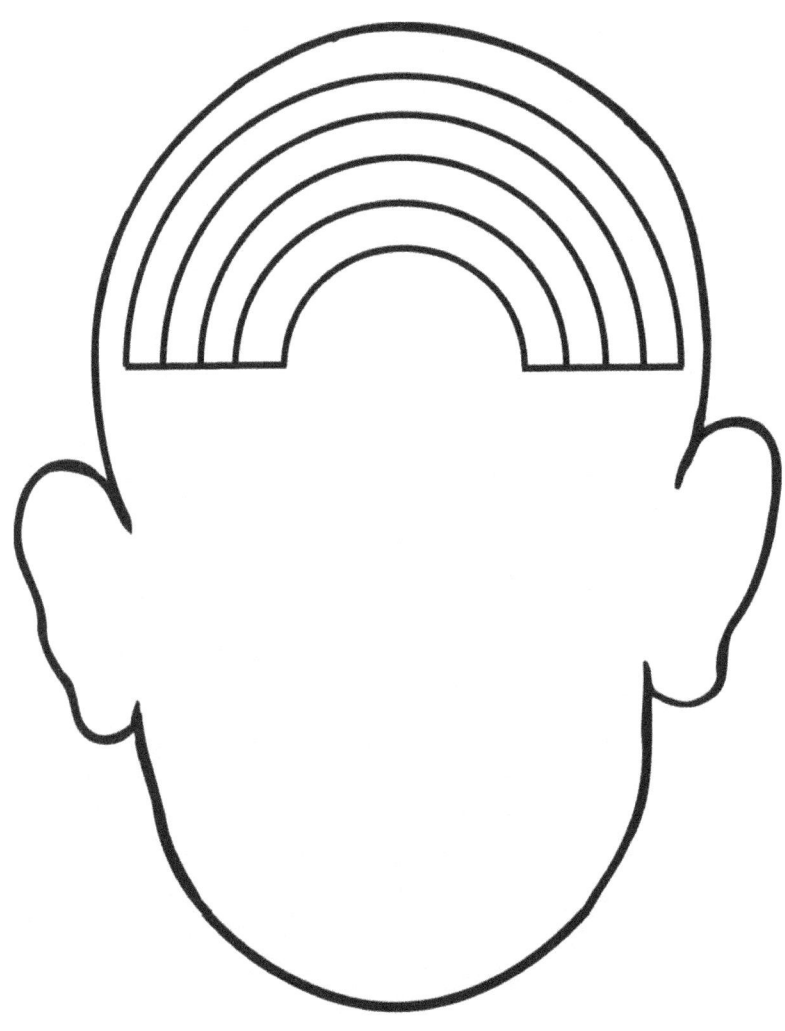

7th Piece of Gold

Everyone has four sub-personalities, with some colours 'shining' brighter than others.

Each of our four sub-personalities is equally important.

Successful people understand how to utilise their strengths and work on their limitations.

8

Use the Click! Colours to Understand Others

'For my thoughts are not your thoughts, neither are your ways my ways.'

Isaiah

'I know you are all fascinated with the Click! Colour Spectrum you have compiled on yourselves, but now it is time to explore the behaviour of others,' Leica stated, refocusing their attention to her next slide.

> **Step 2. Understand Others**
> Who are they - really?
> And why do they behave the way they do?

'Even when we understand our own rainbow, it's our interaction with other people that seems to either light up our life or make our days miserable. How many times have you thought to yourself, "Why do I click with some people and clash with others?"' she challenged.

'How often are we frustrated, annoyed or simply amused by the things other people say or do? Why do some people fuss over which way around the toilet paper goes onto a dispenser? Why do some people cry at movies, while others can sit impassively watching the same film? How can someone simply walk into a car yard and walk out 30 minutes later with a new sports car which they had only seen once? And what is with these people who can analyse charts for months before investing in a fast-moving stock market?' she continued.

'How much do we really know about these people who we work closely with, form friendships with or even make our partners for life? We often take people for granted – at work and at home. We don't really know these people who we are spending so much of our life with, and who are so critical to our success and happiness,' she said, obtaining their total attention.

'Who am I? Who are you? are the most powerful questions we need to ask,' she asserted.

'So, let's start by describing some of the behaviours that may annoy or frustrate you,' Leica suggested. 'But without using judgmental terms,' she added, looking at Bert and Yuri.

Yuri immediately looked at Gail and said, 'Gail sometimes frustrates me because she goes into too much detail. I just want to discuss the big picture. I get annoyed at Gail pointing out little things I may have missed, or risks and practicalities that I haven't considered.'

He smiled and continued, 'I am now seeing that perhaps if I had listened more to Gail, she might have saved me from making some silly mistakes by pointing out details I might have missed.'

'Thanks, Yuri,' responded Gail. 'I guess I should also pay more attention to your ideas – no matter how silly they may seem to me – as you seem to be much more creative and intuitive than I am. You often see what I call problems as great opportunities.'

'Yes, you are both right,' said Rose in her soft, easy-to-listen-to voice. 'If we all sought to truly understand each other and respect each other's opinions, instead of arguing all the time, we would be much happier. We would also be a much better team if we listened to all viewpoints rather than just trying to get our own voices heard,' she continued.

'I hate to admit it, but after analysing what I have just seen and heard, I agree,' added Bert. 'I thought that all of you were not quite up to my level of intelligence, and that was the reason you couldn't see the logic in what I was espousing. But now I realise that you are all intelligent people; it's just that you are different from me.'

'WOW!' they all exclaimed in a chorus. 'Now we know that nothing is wrong with anyone else, nor us. We are all simply the result of different personalities, backgrounds, and experiences.'

'You know what? I think you've got it!' Leica exclaimed as her next slide flashed proudly on the screen.

> I'm OK.
>
> And so are you!

8th Piece of Gold

There is nothing wrong with people who don't think and act the same way as we do.

Our brains are just 'wired' differently, which makes us see life through our own unique Rainbow.

Checkpoint 4

Before you go any further, we need to recognise that while the Click! Colour Cards provide a simple, powerful framework for understanding yourself and others, they should be used with care!

Beware the Two Red Flags!

Human behaviour is incredibly complex, so we need to highlight Two Red Flags to watch out for as you explore yourself and others with the Click! Colours. These Red Flags alert you to other underlying complexities – which when combined with your knowledge of the Click! Colours – will boost your success.

The First Red Flag

Stereotyping and Generalisations

People are a complex mix of all four colours, so beware of stereotyping individuals. Most stereotypes are based on invalid assumptions and generalisations which reduce our ability to appreciate and leverage diversity.

The Second Red Flag

External Factors also Influence Behaviour

Human behaviour is not driven by personality alone. Everyone, regardless of their Click! Colour Spectrum, will also be influenced by the environment they are in. Other factors like culture, family, friends, work, past experiences, or peer group expectations and the situation you are in can influence behaviour.

Read on as our four characters explore the Two Red Flags for themselves…

9
Beware of Stereotyping and Generalisations

(The First Red Flag)

'All generalisations are false, including this one!'

Mark Twain

Suddenly, Bert stood up, which made the others hold their breath in dreaded anticipation. They feared he may walk out of the workshop after all.

'Look, don't get me wrong, I think this is great stuff because it's helping me understand people,' said Bert. 'But I've been thinking.'

'You've been thinking, that's what's wrong with you!' interrupted Yuri, before catching himself and apologising to Bert for interrupting and being judgmental – again!

'Okay, what have you been thinking?' they all chirped in chorus.

'Well,' continued Bert, 'this all seems too simplistic. And it doesn't explain why some people seem different in different situations.'

'Can you give us an example of what you mean?' asked Leica, in an effort to help remove the confused looks on the others' faces.

'Yes,' said Bert. 'For example, sometimes Gail can appear quite messy. Like her desk is often full of scattered paper and reports.'

'Oh, but that's only because I haven't had time to tidy them up,' Gail explained. 'And while I can handle some chaos at times, it needs to be organised chaos. Plus, I need to know that the world will be put back in order at some stage. I always get around to tidying my desk once I have completed the other 20 tasks on my checklist,' she added.

'Okay, but how does Yuri explain the detailed project chart he presented to our board of directors showing his grand plan for expanding our business? I thought Yuri was meant to be big on ideas but short on detail?' Bert continued.

'That's easy,' replied Yuri. 'I painstakingly built that chart because I knew the board would be scared of the scale of my dreams for the business. I thought I would alleviate their fears by showing them step-by-step how it could be achieved over time with gradual changes rather than the big bang approach I used for the last proposal. I didn't want to be rejected again.'

'So, Bert, I think you are trying to complicate things again by over-analysing what we are learning,' suggested Yuri, who just wanted to get back into the fun 'Rainbow' exercise again.

'Hold on,' said Rose, coming to Bert's defence. 'I feel that Bert might have a point. If we go back home, and to work, thinking that these four coloured cards are going to change the world, we might get very disillusioned when they don't always explain someone's behaviour.'

'Excellent!' exclaimed Leica. 'You really are a great mix of people. Just listening to your discussions provides an enormous insight into your personalities. Bert is analysing this learning experience, and rightly so. He, like all of us, wants to get the most out of it. Yuri is starting to get a little frustrated because he would like us to keep it high level and fun and not get down into the weeds. Gail has been taking notes and glancing down at our agenda because she doesn't want to miss anything. She is also getting a little concerned that we are behind schedule and might run out of time at the end of the day. And did you all notice how Rose came to the defence of Bert because the team was not seeking to understand what he was saying, but debating with him and almost dismissing his concerns?'

Yuri responded in his usual excitable tone. 'And guess what? That's exactly how we respond at work. From now on I am going to put more conscious effort into really listening,' he offered. 'Tell me, Bert, what is the key point you are making?'

'Thanks, Yuri.' Bert smiled. 'I am actually making two key points. One is that, while these four colour cards seem to be a very powerful tool for understanding yourself and others, they don't explain why some other logical or analytical people are – in my opinion – very different from me. For example, Belinda Smart in our IT department would definitely have this Blue card as her top card. Her brain would eat mine up when it comes to analysing and problem-solving. Yet she can frustrate even me the way she rationalises everything, including the IT budget. This annoys me just as much as Rose when she wants me to express how I feel about an issue rather than just accepting the figures I give her.'

'My second point is the variance in behaviour I have noticed in people when they are at work as opposed to outside work,' Bert continued. 'Remember that social event we had last month? Well, I was watching Yuri get quite emotional over a story he was being told by Rose about her mother's illness. And Yuri seemed to be really listening, which I thought was out of character for him,' Bert said.

'Brilliant,' responded Leica. 'Sounds like you are ready to explore the implications of what we are learning in more depth. As you have astutely observed, people are more complex than four coloured cards. Lots of factors affect how we all behave.

'So, let's learn about the "Two Red Flags" which we all need to keep in mind when using the Click! Colours.

I deliberately call these Red Flags, as they warn us against being amateur psychologists. And they remind us of how complex humans are compared to the models and tools we use to describe them.' Leica flashed up her next slide, summarising the Two Red Flags.

> **Red Flag 1:** Stereotyping and Generalisations
>
> **Red Flag 2:** External Factors Influence Behaviour

'Let me elaborate,' she continued, as she explained each Red Flag in detail.

Red Flag 1: Stereotyping and Generalisations.

'The Click! Colour Cards and our Click! Colour Spectrum give us a great framework to work with, but we must recognise that they are not a definitive description of personality and behaviour. They are very useful tools for helping you understand yourself and why you behave in certain ways, and they help you understand other people. Their strength lies in their simplicity and easy practical application. But they will be even more valuable if you understand their limitations as well,' Leica stressed.

'Our natural tendency is to try to put people into certain categories. This is natural because our world is already so complex and hard to understand. Putting complex creatures such as other people into convenient boxes helps us cope – or so we think. We also tend to generalise and stereotype people according to the colour of their skin, religious beliefs, or even their country of origin. And while someone's background, beliefs and origin are all important, they do not provide the whole picture. Just like the four personality colour cards, we seek ways of making sense out of the vast, complex array of different thinking and behaviour we encounter and observe,' she continued.

'But it is precisely this rich complexity of human nature that provides the greatest benefit to successful living. Thus, making the effort to truly understand others, rather than just wishing they would understand us, is where the biggest gains in life are waiting to be made,' she said.

'Instead of labelling people Red, Green, Blue or Yellow we need to seek to understand the whole person. How does their "Rainbow" look compared to ours and others, and what does this mean when communicating, team-working or building relationships with them?' she asked.

'Then, it can be extremely useful to shuffle the four coloured cards, and explore all the macro-variations that make up different people before attempting a deeper exploration of each unique individual,' she suggested, as another thought-provoking slide appeared on the screen.

> 'There is nothing so unequal as the equal treatment of unequals.'
>
> Kenneth Blanchard

'Yes, I like the idea of using the colour cards like a deck of playing cards. We could examine issues through the eyes of others by shuffling the cards and putting different cards on top. We could then explore how someone of that colour preference would react to the problem,' suggested Yuri, who was getting a little impatient and wanted more interaction.

Gail then spotted an opening to add, 'And I will feel more comfortable with these cards now that I know I can look at them in different sequences. Then, if I make a mistake with my initial choices, I can simply experiment with the order of preference until I feel comfortable with my choice,' she shared.

'I agree that we need to give more thought to the complexity of human behaviour,' added Bert, 'as I think there is much more to my Click! Colour Spectrum than meets the eye,' he hypothesised.

'I'm just glad we all agree that stereotyping and labelling people should be avoided,' remarked Rose. 'I know I get upset when people say I'm too soft and gullible. They don't really understand the whole me. They would be shocked to see the warrior side of me at the Protect Nature protest marches I attend,' she added with a smile.

'Great, looks like we all strongly agree that stereotyping and generalisations get in the way of truly appreciating and using the complexity inherent in all of us,' Leica summarised. 'So, let's move on to the second Red Flag,' she suggested.

9th Piece of Gold

Stereotyping, generalisations and inaccurate assumptions reduce our ability to appreciate and leverage diversity.

10

External Factors Also Influence Behaviour

(The Second Red Flag)

'We are powerfully influenced by our surroundings, our immediate context and the personalities of those around us.'

Malcolm Gladwell

'The Second Red Flag simply reminds us that nobody lives in a vacuum,' Leica explained. 'All behaviour is to some extent influenced by the people, culture, systems, rules – written and unwritten, norms, beliefs and the situation we find ourselves in,' she continued.

'Have you ever noticed how some people behave very differently at a fancy dress party from how they do at work?' Leica asked.

'Yes indeed!' said Bert as he glanced at Yuri.

Leica continued her questioning without breaking stride.

'And have you ever observed children who appear to be absolute angels at a friend's place, yet act like little devils at home? And has someone you know as being meek and humble transformed into a dictator when put in charge of a yacht, orchestra, or sports team? Or have you ever talked to a hero who claims they're not naturally brave, but were forced into heroic action by the crisis they faced? And has the same person you were having a laugh with over lunch ever transformed into a hard-nosed profit-seeking missile when you walked into the boardroom meeting? And have you encountered a team which appeared to be hopeless one year, only to become champions when the coach and team leader were changed the next?' she concluded, as they all nodded agreement.

'Well, all of this seemingly incongruous behaviour is largely a result of the interplay between individuals and the environment that surrounds them – real or perceived,' Leica explained.

'Kurt Lewin, a psychologist from 1890–1947, explained this phenomenon in his equation **B** = **f** (**P, E**), which symbolises his proposition that human Behaviour is a function of both the People and Environment they are in,' Leica continued, as she flashed her own simplified, yet no less powerful, equation on the screen.

> **Behaviour (B) = People (P) + Environment (E)**
>
> **(Nature + Nurture)**

'Thus, anyone who leads people, wants to create a high-performance team, desires a better relationship, longs for a more harmonious home life, wishes to be a better parent, or just wants people to behave in a more positive manner, should think long and hard about this simple equation,' she stressed. 'It reminds us that human behaviour is a function of two things. Firstly, the People – their personality and the genetic make-up that influences how they behave – and secondly, the Environment they are operating in – or perceive they are operating in,' she continued.

'That is why people behave differently in different situations. Calm people can be made to panic, naughty children guided into good behaviour, poorly performing teams transformed into high-performing ones, fearful people made to feel safe – all by manipulating the environment around them. These external influences include our surroundings, for example: hot–cold, noisy–quiet, active–passive, chaotic–controlled, dangerous–safe and turbulent–calm, and even the personalities of others around us,' she suggested.

'Have you ever noticed how someone you regard as noisy and boisterous can be so calm and quiet when immersed in the sedate environment of a church, monastery or library?

Or how sedate they are when lying in bed reading a book with no distractions? Or how their voice gradually lowers and slows when surrounded by quieter, more introverted people, yet joins in the pace and tone of louder groups?' she asked.

'So, what does this mean for us?' asked Yuri, impatient for quick answers.

'Well, in simple terms it means we should start by identifying the behaviour we want to encourage. We could then create the most positive environment we can to drive this behaviour. For example, if we want everyone in this team to provide input on an equal basis, then we need to provide the environment in which this is likely to happen,' replied Leica.

'I'm not sure I know what you mean,' offered Rose.

'Okay, let me give you an example from my limited exposure to this team,' Leica responded. 'I have already noticed how Yuri sometimes interrupts others to offer his own thoughts. He doesn't mean to be disruptive. In fact, he is genuinely trying to help the team with his insights. But sometimes it means that the person offering the initial idea gets trodden on and feels less inclined to offer more ideas. They start to feel that their input is not valued or that they have been disregarded before they have been fully listened to or understood.'

'Oh, you mean like when I ask the others in this group to just get to the bottom line of what they are saying?' asked Bert.

'Yes,' replied Leica. 'By forcing others to make that leap forward to a logical conclusion, they – unlike you – have to change their thought patterns. This creates discomfort, which acts against them being so forthcoming in future.'

'Wow, I never realised the extent to which we impact on the behaviours of others!' exclaimed Gail.

'Yes. We can really help each other flourish by recognising people's needs and their Click! Colour Spectrum,' answered Leica.

'For example, respecting the need for Blue-dominant people like Bert to understand the logic behind a problem means the group should try to build some rationale into their discussions,' she said.

'And Reds like to have space to communicate people-issues. So don't clog up every meeting and conversation with data and business issues,' she advised.

'Greens, on the other hand, need the detailed data required to feel comfortable with decisions. So, you can help them by being organised and fully prepared,' Leica continued.

'And Yellows crave permission to explore wild ideas and go off on tangents,' Leica added.

'Maybe we should even actively seek opportunities for each of us to practise different ways of thinking about issues?' said Rose.

'Yes, like we said before about shuffling different coloured cards and stepping into others' shoes,' added Gail, referring to her notes.

'That sounds very creative and fun. Well done, Gail!' responded Yuri.

'I agree. We would be much more productive as a group if we leveraged our diversity,' added Bert.

'Yes, to all of those suggestions,' responded Leica. 'But please don't get too serious about all this. Remember that the best teams balance "Excellence with Fun",' she continued, as she flashed up her next slide on the screen.

> The best teams balance excellence with fun.

'So, please do shuffle the cards, play with them, explore all the variations and continue your learning using a "child's mindset" – naïve, fun, persistent and open-minded,' Leica reinforced.

10th Piece of Gold

Our behaviour is not only influenced by personality types but also by:

- Experiences, beliefs and values
- The situation we are in
- The people we are with

Providing an environment that is conducive to all personality types will boost results.

11
How We See Ourselves Is Not How Others See Us

'We don't see things as they are. We see things as we are.'

Anais Nin

'I would like to ask a question now, if I may?' asked Rose, in a gentle yet assertive tone which grabbed the group's attention.

'Sure, go ahead,' responded Leica.

'My question is this,' Rose started. 'How come some people seem to be acting out roles no matter what environment they are in?' she continued. 'Even though I am quite good at picking people, some are much harder to read than others,' she concluded.

'Great question.' Leica agreed, as she surveyed the faces in the group to elicit a response.

'Perhaps it's because some people don't really know themselves?' suggested Yuri.

'Or maybe they do think they know themselves, but would rather be viewed differently by others,' added Bert.

'You mean they aspire to be somebody different?' queried Yuri.

'Yeah, like if Gail wanted to appear more outlandish, extroverted and entrepreneurial, she might start acting a bit more like you, Yuri,' Bert suggested, in a logical yet jovial manner.

'No, I disagree,' Gail burst out.

'Oh, I don't think Bert meant you exactly,' Rose quickly intervened, trying to diffuse the situation. 'I think he was talking about people in general,' she added.

But it was Leica who once again came to the rescue of the group.

'I think what you are all starting to explore is yet another complexity that sometimes masks our true personality,' she suggested. 'You see, even when we understand our Click! Colour Spectrum and the environment influencing behaviour, we still have to sometimes contend with what I call "The Three Faces" of people. The Three Faces are the person we really are, the person we would like others to see us as being, and the person others see when they interact with us,' she explained, as her summary slide appeared.

HOW WE SEE OURSELVES IS NOT HOW OTHERS SEE US

> 'If you could see yourself as others see you, you would probably have your eyes examined!'
>
> Who am I really?
> Who do others see?
> Who would I like to be?

'So, please understand how important it is to accept and love who you really are, rather than trying to fit into some social or team norm. No single colour card is more or less important, powerful or valuable than any other. And no Click! Colour Spectrum combination is better than any other,' she continued. 'The real power in knowing yourself is the gift of choice it gives you. You can choose to live within your comfort zone and build upon your natural preferences – be they Red, Green, Yellow or Blue. You can also consciously develop the colours that are less natural for you,' she added, as another thought-provoking slide appeared.

> Be yourself, but be aware.

'Nothing is stopping a natural Blue from developing his or her emotional Red side. It just takes awareness, understanding and conscious effort. Yes, even deep Blues can truly listen to what the other person is trying to express without constantly analysing and trying to solve their problems,' she suggested, as Bert nodded in agreement. 'And yes, Greens can take risks and be more impulsive if they choose to. Just as Yellows can pay attention to detail by consciously focusing their attention onto one thing at a time, and by using more self-discipline,' she continued, as Gail and Yuri smiled at each other.

'And just because a Red's natural bias will be towards people-issues, doesn't mean that they can't be just as business and task focused as anyone else,' she added.

'The Click! Colour Cards help us understand who we really are,' she stressed. 'They illuminate how others may see us and can help us grow as the person we want to be,' Leica concluded.

11th Piece of Gold

How we see ourselves is not always how others see us. There are three sides to all of us:

- The person we are.
- The person we want to be.
- The person people perceive us to be.

Click! Colours help us understand how people see us.

12

Successful People Know Themselves and Apply This Knowledge

> '*Knowing others is intelligence; knowing yourself is true wisdom.*'
>
> Lao Tzu

'This is so exciting,' chirped Yuri, immediately lifting the energy of the group. 'Now I know why I often thought that the world was full of boring stick-in-the-muds,' he chuckled.

'Yeah, and I thought people like you were just dreamers,' smiled Gail, as she held up the Yellow card to ensure others wouldn't be mistaken about who she meant.

'And I am pleased to admit that I no longer think the world is full of people who can't use logic to solve their own problems,' laughed Bert.

'Yes, you folks really do have a heart of gold,' Rose added. 'It just doesn't shine as openly in some of us,' she added with a glint in her eye.

'That's fantastic!' exclaimed Leica. 'But, just understanding and appreciating differences – powerful as that may be – is nothing compared to putting that learning into action,' she stated, as her next slide appeared.

> **Step 3. Understand the Implications**
>
> How can understanding each other help us in our relationships, teamwork and life in general?

'So, let's now use this knowledge of Self and Others by identifying the key **Strengths** we can build upon, and then exploring the **Limitations** we need to overcome to succeed in all aspects of life,' Leica asserted.

'Knowing which colour card is most like you, and therefore, the most natural for you, provides hints to your possible **Strengths**. Acknowledging and building upon these strengths will fast-track your success. It allows you to focus on and train what you are potentially very good at,' she advised.

'Yes,' agreed Rose. 'We are often so immersed in our failings and supposed weaknesses we lose sight of everyone's good points, including our own!' she concluded.

'So how do we start?' asked Bert, as he surprised himself by sensing that the others were now eager to explore their abilities in more depth.

'A good first step is to revisit the colour card that you believed was most like you and list on a flip chart what you believe are the Top 3 attributes which you could build into core strengths,' Leica Rainbow instructed.

Bert walked straight over to a flip chart next to the Blue Wall Chart and forced himself to read its contents – this time with the most open, non-judgmental attitude he could summon. This is what he came up with:

Bert
Top card Blue: Analyser
Potential Strengths

1. I like to analyse everything and enjoy problem-solving using mathematical / scientific methods. This natural tendency could help the team integrate logic into team decisions.

2. Making decisions based on facts comes naturally for me (one of my favourite sayings is 'prescription without diagnosis is malpractice').

3. Logic-based change is OK (even if it means breaking the rules) but change for change-sake is just silly. I could help the team move past emotional barriers to change by helping them see the logical benefit.

Yuri had also already completed his 'Top 3' list, which he considered to be very impressive. This is how his flip chart read:

Yuri
Top card Yellow: Playmaker
Potential Strengths

1. I enjoy taking risks when others may hesitate. My favourite saying is 'Just do it!' This 'high-risk' tolerance can help the team make quicker decisions where the downside risks are minimal.

2. Fast, intuitive decision making comes naturally for me. 'A quick decision is a good decision' I say. I also like to 'think outside the box'.

3. Flexibility and adaptability are a good thing in my book - change is exciting, not threatening.

Gail straightened the Green Wall Chart before she proceeded to list her perceived strengths. This is what she wrote:

Gail
Top card Green: Safekeeper
Potential Strengths

1. I am a 'Natural' risk assessor. I often see risks and possible dangers where others (like Yuri) only see 'opportunities' - so I can save people and organisations from making costly mistakes.

2. I tend towards 'practical' decisions that are grounded in 'the rules' and what makes sense rather than 'wild' schemes. I like to point out that there are rules and we should follow them.

3. I am definitely organised, dependable and will follow through and complete most tasks. This natural tendency could help teams complete tasks before running off to other projects.

Rose seemed deep in thought as she carefully crafted her key points. Her flip chart looked like this:

Rose
Top card Red: Carer
Potential Strengths

1. For me 'risk-taking is okay', but I am careful to consider the impact on people and the environment. This can help the team make better decisions where people issues are important.

2. I naturally include some emotional component (people or feelings) in my decision making, and trust what I 'feel' is the right decision.

3. I think people need to be involved in any change process so both their hearts and minds are engaged. So long as no-one gets hurt, change can be good.

Checkpoint 5

Now it is your turn to recognise your strengths. Just like our colourful characters, revisit your top card. What are the top three attributes that you can build into core strengths?

Name: _____
Top card: _____

Potential Strengths

1.

2.

3.

'Great work,' praised Leica as she surveyed their flip charts. 'Now that you recognise your strengths, you can maximise the leverage you get from them.'

'Now, let's see if the colour card you chose as least like you can provide some equally powerful insights. This card will reveal limitations that can provide enormous personal growth opportunities when overcome,' she continued.

'So, let's explore what impact your bottom card could have on your success in life,' she challenged, as they walked to the flip charts next to the colour they had decided was least like them.

Yuri was first to begin, although this time his list took longer to complete as he struggled to identify possible limitations he may need to overcome.

Yuri
Bottom card: Green
Possible Limitations

1. I sometimes miss important details, especially in long complex written proposals/agreements. This is probably because I get bored easily and can be distracted by other more fun things to do.

2. I tend to have too many projects on the go and may frustrate others by leaving projects unfinished.

CHECKPOINT 5   113

Gail surprised herself with the ease of this task. She had no difficulty pinpointing her possible faults.

Gail
Bottom card: Yellow
Possible Limitations

1. I sometimes take too long evaluating possible risks and miss some great opportunities.

2. I tend to get stuck in a rut and wonder why life isn't more interesting.

Rose also found this exercise relatively easy, yet a little unpleasant as she listed some of her perceived limitations.

Rose
Bottom card: Blue
Possible Limitations

1. I experience remorse more often than most, as my decisions are not always well thought out and analysed. I often make decisions because I feel it is the 'right thing' to do.

2. I struggle with financial, mathematical and scientific endeavours. Although I recognise they are important, they don't really appeal to me.

CHECKPOINT 5   115

Of all the participants, Bert found this assignment the hardest of all. Finally, after much analysis, he admitted to himself that his key limitations were:

Bert
Bottom card: Red
Possible Limitations

1. I could be perceived as cold and even heartless, especially by Reds as I focus on hard facts and logic to the exclusion of people issues and Right Brain creativity.

2. I tend to miss a lot of personal cues from others due to the lack of an emotional antennae.

'Wow!' exclaimed Yuri as they discussed each flip chart. 'This is really powerful. I guess the beauty of knowing this stuff is that we can now do something about it,' he suggested.

'Yes, and we now have some facts to work with, so we are less likely to make a mistake,' added Gail.

'More importantly, I am now beginning to understand why some people annoy and even frustrate me,' Bert admitted.

'And how I might sometimes annoy or frustrate others who are not like me,' he added.

'That's a great revelation, Bert. I think this could really help us become a much more harmonious team,' Rose reflected.

Leica was delighted with both their output and their honesty. 'I am so pleased with our progress,' she stated. 'It looks like you are now ready to explore the practical applications of this knowledge in your workplace.'

Checkpoint 6

Knowing your limitations is equally powerful. They can provide opportunities for personal growth. Look at your bottom card. What is the impact of your limitations on your growth and success?

Name: _____

Top card: _____
Possible Limitations

Putting it into Action:

Applying the Knowledge at Work

Surprisingly, Bert jumped in before Yuri could, and suggested that they should 'shuffle' the cards and place themselves in other people's shoes.

'How do we do that?' asked Gail.

'Well,' Bert continued, 'take our meetings, for example. Perhaps if Yuri had to organise the meeting and take the minutes, he could put the Green card in front of him. This would encourage him to be on time and pay attention to the specific action points required. Gail could place the Yellow card in front of her to encourage some out of the box ideas. Rose could look at the Blue card as a reminder of the fact that we need to keep the bottom line dollar in perspective. And I could look at the Red card to remind me that I need to seek out the people issues that need to be discussed.'

'Great start,' agreed the others. 'How about each of us making a personal pact to support each other when we get back to work?' they suggested in unison.

Leica smiled as she listened to their suggestions. She was confident that they had taken the first tentative steps towards becoming a great team. Yet, at the same time she was somewhat apprehensive as she also knew that – like any life-changing event – they would often revert to their old ways.

'Looks like a good time to take our coffee break,' Leica suggested, hoping that they had built enough momentum to sustain their curiosity about each other well into the future. 'When we get back, we'll investigate how we can apply our newfound knowledge back at work.'

12th Piece of Gold

Knowing the make up of our own personalities helps us become a better 'whole person' by enabling us to capitalise on our strengths and work on our limitations.

13

Use Click! Colours to Boost Success

Diversity when understood and used creates exceptional results.

Leica Rainbow was astounded. She couldn't believe what she saw when she walked back into the room. Gail had got back early from the coffee break and had arranged all the chairs neatly in a row. She had put everything back in order, even straightening the wall charts, and was handing out Strategic Planning folders.

Yuri was late, and Bert had his calculator out working on a spreadsheet.

'What is wrong with them?' Leica thought, exasperated. She was shocked at how quickly they had reverted to old habits.

Developing an understanding of people's behaviour is one thing, but changing old habits is another, she reminded herself. Changing the thinking and behaviour of individuals won't happen instantly, and there are bound to be a few setbacks in the process. As Dolly Parton said, we need to experience a bit of 'rain' before we experience the full benefits of the rainbow. Change requires commitment and persistence. So, let's be persistent she thought.

'Right, can we get back to our planning workshop now?' Gail suggested as Yuri entered the room talking to Rose. 'According to the agenda we are 15 minutes behind schedule,' Gail noted.

'Hold on,' interjected Rose, with an unusual degree of assertiveness. 'Let's not jump straight back into our comfort zones. Continuing to explore each other's personal "rainbow" and how we can use this knowledge will be far more valuable than just writing a Strategic Plan. Besides, we can always write the plan back at work. But I can't see us becoming a high-performance team without more coaching on how to improve our interpersonal relationships.'

'Yes, Rose is right,' supported Bert as he put down his calculator. 'This is powerful stuff. Just imagine all the problems and heartache we could have all avoided if only we understood each other. Plus, I am keen to discover how I can use this stuff at home as well.'

'Hmm, I suppose you are right,' admitted Gail. 'Perhaps this colour stuff is more important than my silly agenda,' she smiled as she discarded her folder. 'And I would love to be able to use it outside of work as well,' she agreed.

'Okay,' responded Leica. 'Let's start with those of you who have partners. Tell me, are they very different from you? Do they sometimes frustrate you with the way they do things? Would their Click! Colour Spectrum have different colours shining through?' she asked, knowing full well what the answer would be.

Bert started, 'Well I can't speak for other people, but my wife is very different from me. During this exercise I have been thinking about her and decided she would be Red card dominant. Totally different from me. And I would guess that most people would have partners who are very different from them.'

'Yes, most people tell me that the partners they have chosen to share their life with are very different from them. This means that they have different preferred sub-personalities. But why do you think that is?' Leica asked.

'That's simple,' responded Yuri in a flash. 'It's because opposites attract.'

'Yes, but isn't it more about the fact that their strengths are our weaknesses, and their weaknesses are our strengths?' Bert asserted.

'In practical terms it makes sense that you would seek out a partner who has abilities that compensate for your limitations,' added Gail.

'What do you think?' Leica asked, looking at Rose.

'I think it's because the person you choose completes you in some way,' Rose suggested. 'It's almost as if it were meant to be. And you only feel whole when they are around.'

'Yes, great answers from all of you. But, if we all agree that being different can actually be of great benefit in a relationship, why does it cause so many problems?' questioned Leica.

'That's easy. It's because we all think we are right. Therefore, people with differing views are probably wrong,' suggested Yuri.

'Rubbish! I don't think I am right – I KNOW I am right, so therefore everyone else is definitely wrong if they don't agree with my view,' Bert responded with a cheeky grin and an uncommon degree of humour. They all laughed.

'Very funny,' continued Leica, suppressing her laughter. 'Now, do you remember this slide I showed you earlier?' she asked.

> **I'm OK, it's just all of you who have problems!**

'So, bearing in mind what we have just learned, we need to change our mindset to:

> **I'm OK, and guess what -
> so are you!**

'Wow! I can't wait to take these cards back to work and use them on the people in my team. And at home tonight I can explore them with my wife and children,' exclaimed Yuri excitedly. 'They are going to love this stuff!'

'Yes, now I can tell my workmates and family exactly what is wrong with them!' added Bert, with a relieved look on his face.

'Wait a minute,' Rose said. 'How will others feel about being psychoanalysed by us? I know I would feel uncomfortable if someone started telling me who I am,' she offered.

'I agree,' said Gail. 'Running out of here and confronting others could be a big risk,' she cautioned. 'But if we don't use this knowledge and share with others, how will we ever build truly great relationships?'

'Oh, stop putting up barriers all the time,' Yuri said, expressing frustration at others upsetting his grand plan to use this newfound knowledge beyond the boundaries of the workshop.

'Yes, logically these cards are of limited use if they only reside with me,' Bert supported. 'Surely the more people who understand their Click! Colours, the more successful all of us will be?' he said.

'I agree entirely. We just need to use this newfound knowledge and tools correctly, so we get the maximum benefit for both ourselves and others,' Leica suggested. 'So let me give you some advice on how best to use these cards outside this workshop environment.

'Firstly, all of us should put ourselves in the other person's shoes. They have not attended this workshop and so have not experienced the same journey of discovery that you have. They may also have had bad experiences of others trying to "tell" them things or zealously forcing new ideas on them. Also, think about how different personalities are likely to react to someone approaching them with a set of coloured cards like an evangelist,' she warned.

'Blues are likely to cross their arms and dismiss you as fluffy from the moment you open your mouth. Greens will start taking notes but soon disengage when no apparent order or sequence emerges. Yellows may get excited about the Yellow card but are unlikely to fully explore the other cards and may dismiss the true value of these cards, and Reds may simply become upset that you are not taking the time to truly understand them and are treating them like an object. So, instead of confronting people with this newfound knowledge and tools, find ways for them to discover their own Rainbow. For example, simply leave the cards somewhere they will find them (on a table, in the kitchen/lunchroom), and let them start to explore the Rainbow for themselves,' Leica suggested. 'After all, learning is more fun when we are involved in the learning process, rather than when others try to do it to us,' she advised.

'Okay, that makes sense,' they replied. 'Now, what about us? How can we make use of what we have learned?'

'Good question,' Leica responded. 'Let's finish this workshop with some ideas on "Where and How" this knowledge can be put to best use. I have compiled some key areas where personality has a major impact. So, let's identify our discussion points on each flip chart.'

Leica Rainbow then took the Spectrum team through a process highlighting how they could apply their knowledge of the Click! Colours in their **Relationships, Family, Teamwork, Leadership, Decision Making, Change** and **Personal Productivity**.

Here is a summary of their thoughts:

Relationships

Great relationships are the ONE common essential factor for emotional and financial success in all aspects of life.

The key to successful relationships is to first love yourself, your abilities, your lovable traits, and accept your foibles knowing that you are constantly seeking to improve – but are not perfect. Then appreciate other people – their strengths, uniqueness, and inevitable flaws. All of which is extremely hard without some knowledge and tools to help us recognise how our own personality shapes our behaviour, and how the personality of others influences their behaviour towards the world and us.

Seek to understand what is important and less important to others and why. Don't assume that what is important to you is equally fascinating to others. (For example, Reds don't want to talk business and money as much as Blues might. Greens may be reluctant to do something impulsive and risky that Yellows might view as fun and exciting.)

In all relationships, it is important to step out of your own shoes occasionally and walk in the shoes of others. Appreciate the different ways others see the world and accept that there isn't just one way to live.

Many close, long-term relationships involve people who are opposite to each other (Yellows with Green partners, Blues married to Reds and so on). In these cases, the partner or very close friend or associate should be viewed as completing you in some way. Together, you can benefit from all four sub-personalities and whole-brain thinking – BUT – only if both parties are willing to look past their own biases.

Family

All families are a diverse mix of personalities, which is one reason why they can cause such drama, love and happiness.

Partners and children are all different, even if they share some common personality preferences, so be careful about stereotyping others. Try to understand their personal Rainbow rather than thinking, "They just don't make sense."

Most natural Greens in a family tend to be more practical and focused than natural Yellows, who seek more fun and are easily bored. Thus, some Yellow children may seem naughty and hyperactive. Before you start labelling them, consider that they may simply be seeking more challenge and stimulation.

Allow yourself to adapt to the preferences that different family members may have; for example, you may wish to play more creative/active games with Yellows and engage in more methodical tasks like building things with Greens. Allow Reds space to express their emotions and encourage Blues to exercise their minds playing games like chess and Scrabble.

Just enjoy the diversity in your family, without being too judgmental. Remember, there is nothing wrong with them; they are just different.

Teamwork

All colours contribute greatly to teamwork, but the greatest benefit is gained when others understand how to leverage both their own ability as well as that of others who are very different from them.

Reds aid teams by reminding them that everything comes down to people. The best technology, systems, marketing, production lines, and service agreements are worthless unless you have the people to design, build, operate, and back them up. That's why Reds can often be heard talking about values, teamwork, harmony, and other people issues.

However, Reds can add even more value to the team by stepping outside their comfort zone and being more assertive when the team needs it. Stern words emanating from the mouth of a Red can have great impact. Rather than avoiding conflict, Reds can contribute to team success by taking more action, especially when the team needs to wake up and realise that its performance is not acceptable; a hard thing for a Red to do but well worth doing, both for the benefit of the team and the Red's own personal growth.

Blues, in contrast, can learn a lot from the way Reds appreciate that the team is not composed of Human Resources, but rather, people; people who are diverse, unique and have talents which the team needs to optimise. So, Blues who can step aside from their analytical thought processes for a minute and truly sense the team – its mood, morale, underlying emotional currents, and sense of interdependence – add enormous value.

In a similar way, Greens can benefit the team and themselves by being willing to venture outside their comfort zone and risk throwing impulsive, even out of the box ideas into the mix of discussion when the team is brainstorming ways to improve. This out of the box behaviour, combined with being the natural Safekeeper (who supports the team in seeking detailed follow-up actions) adds great value to the team or family.

Most high Yellows will tell you that they are already the biggest contributor to the team's success. After all, they seem to be the ones who come up with all the great ideas, only to be shot down by Blues who ask: "Where is the business case to support that?"; or Reds who gently remind them that such a grand scheme would impact on a lot of people who have only just settled into their current jobs; or those pesky Greens who come up with: We couldn't possibly do that. Haven't you read page 97 of the current Standard Operating Procedure? And besides, if it ain't broke, why fix it?

The breakthrough for Yellows in team contribution occurs when they add key questions to their impulsive thought processes like: 'What would the cost/benefit of that idea look like? Will it improve the way we currently do things without adding unmanageable risk?'

Leadership

Leadership is not just the domain of people placed in formal positions of authority. Everyone faces leadership scenarios at various stages of their lives – within families, organisations, the community and with friends. Influencing and engaging others to watch a particular movie is a simple form of leadership. And like every form of human interaction, knowing what "makes you tick" and what "turns others on" is essential for effective leadership. So, this time let's look at leadership through the eyes of the followers.

Blues are unlikely to be swayed by emotive arguments such as "You must come and see this movie with me; it's a real tear-jerker." The leader has more chance using a more logical reason like, "This movie will help your professional development as it explores right brain aspects that you could learn a lot from."

Reds, of course, can be attracted by the emotional connection to something the group sets as a goal. Even the downsizing of a company's workforce, a turn-off for most Reds who hate to see people lose their jobs, can be effectively communicated by the leader by using terms like, "Regrettable as this action is, we must reduce our staff numbers for the company to survive. This will also allow us to continue benefiting the people who rely on our services, the community and charities we support, the people who supply products and services to us and the people we can still employ under the new structure."

To engage Greens in your leadership vision, it had better include some practical details, not just fluffy jargon. Exactly "What is going to happen, Where, by Whom and When" is a great start, especially when backed by a step-by-step process and risk management plan.

Yellows prefer the inspirational leader. 'Just paint me a picture of your vision, and if it is aligned with mine – or even more interesting and exciting than mine – then I will follow you!' they exclaim.

Decision Making

Understanding your preferred thinking habits – and what may annoy or frustrate you – will make your decision making exponentially more powerful.

Yellows often enjoy quick, sometimes impulsive decision making and may avoid – or even fight against – using a logical, analytical process that they call analysis paralysis. For Yellows, integrating more analysis, attention to detail and how the outcome will impact on others will boost their success.

Blues regard proper analysis as essential to logical decision making. Where they fall down is by not sensing how their decisions impact on others, and taking too long and missing breakthroughs by resisting any non-rational solutions.

Reds are different again, often basing decisions on how they feel in their heart of hearts, especially when it is a very important decision like getting married, buying a house or changing jobs. Reds could benefit by giving more weight to the logical/practical possibilities, which may not feel right at first but are better solutions in the long run.

Greens regard impulsive decisionmaking as too risky. They struggle to understand why anyone would not use a defined process to ensure risks are identified – the facts are known – and the final decision is not rushed. Thus, Greens can miss great opportunities unless they consciously balance the Risk-Reward equation.

Change

The Lippitt-Knoster Model for Complex Change provides a powerful lens through which to view successful change management. For our four characters, this formula offers the ideal framework for understanding their journey. We have adapted the model slightly, replacing 'skills' and 'incentives' with the catalyst of 'pressure'. Giving the formula:

$$P+V+R+A=C$$

where P= Pressure, V = Vision, R = Resources, A= Action Plan and C=Change

And we can use that equation to gain an insight into why people see change differently.

Yellows will tend to be more interested in change if the vision (V) is exciting. In fact, they may get so immersed in the Grand Vision that they neglect to consider the resources (R) required, the follow-up action (A) steps, or even whether the change is even needed. Rarely will they ask, 'Where is the pressure (P) for this change? Why do we need to do it?'

The first question Blues will ask is, 'Why are we doing this?' They want to know the logic behind the change. They will also ask 'Why do we need it? And where is the Pressure (P) that is driving this variance from the norm?'. Answers to these questions are more important to them than the Grand Vision.

Greens are also healthy sceptics of change. But their primary concern centres around any danger to the status quo. 'If it ain't broke, don't fix it!' is the catch cry of the true Green. Not because they can't see any room for improvement, rather because they see the need for an orderly world and any threat to the current way of doing things is often resisted unless a clear pressure (P) is identified and the specific action (A) steps to achieve the change are scoped out and practical.

Reds, as usual, are more concerned with the impact the change might have on people, relationships and teamwork. They will sometimes surprise others with their resistance to change, but when you dig deeper behind their motives, it often relates to people issues.

For example, a simple office move might elicit unseen passion in the Reds involved if they see the move as a disruption to relationships they have formed and value. Moving them away from a desk where a friend sits feels like a drastic and unwelcome change, even if the Pressure, Vision, Resources, and Actions for the transition have been clearly explained and make sense. If, however, it can be shown that the new office environment will be even more people-friendly than before and that it would benefit others, then Reds will accept change as much as anyone.

So, despite popular belief, people don't resist change per se. They only resist it if the change appears to be no better, or even worse, than their current situation. And they will certainly resist if their own unique perspective of the change is not recognised, respected or catered for. That's why some people are perceived as being negative or obstructive when proponents of the change can only see the upside.

Personal Productivity

All colours, and mixtures of colours, can boost personal productivity by expanding beyond the comfort zones which constrain them.

Yellows are much more effective and productive when they employ some Green traits to complete tasks before getting distracted and moving onto another project or new idea. When Yellows use disciplined planning, and a Blue's logical thought process to think through tasks, they find themselves spending less time misdirected and more time focused on what's important.

Conversely, Greens can reduce the amount of time they spend bogged down in data-gathering or endless detail by adopting more of a Yellow mindset – stepping back, seeing the big picture – and accepting that sometimes 80% complete is okay so long as it delivers the required result.

Similarly, Blues can boost their productivity by avoiding getting trapped into over analysing and accepting that the most important tasks in life do not always follow logical paths. Engaging others (at work or home) to help achieve a common goal is more about understanding what motivates people than any logical dissertation. Blues boost their productivity once they realise you can only achieve so much by yourself. Enlisting others achieves a lot more.

Reds face a very different challenge when it comes to productivity. Their challenge is more about accepting that while people issues are important, sometimes you have to 'let go' and focus on the tasks at hand. This can be particularly tough for Reds as it can mean being more tough-minded at times. This includes not being drawn into long discussions with people who are simply using the Red as a sympathetic sounding board for something that they themselves forget about soon after.

The discussions that took place at each flip chart could have lasted for days as the group realised just how much personality impacts on personal and business life. However, their attention was diverted when Leica Rainbow rang her bell to announce that it was time to wrap up the day.

'Now that you are armed with some great knowledge and ideas, it's time to go and use them.' She started. 'Enjoy playing with the Click! Colour Cards. Have fun with them. Pull them out of your pocket often to continue your journey of understanding yourself and others. Expose others to what you have learned. Leave the cards where others can pick them up and explore them for themselves. And above all, continue to explore the Rainbow in more depth and you will constantly uncover many more secrets to successful living,' she suggested as they concluded for the day.

13th Piece of Gold

Understanding the Click! Colours will boost success in many areas of life including relationships, family, teamwork, leadership, decision making, change management, and personal productivity.

14

Use the Click! Colours to Enhance Relationships at Home

Know yourself and others, and magical relationships will blossom.

Bert caught himself smiling on his drive home from the workshop. He was filled with a sense of relief, as if a huge burden had been lifted from his shoulders. Never before had he felt so relaxed and comfortable about coming home.

For Bert, home life had always seemed a bit of a struggle. Every time his wife came to him with a problem, he offered his best logical solutions or set of options she should consider, yet she rarely took his advice or even thanked him for helping. In fact, she appeared even more dissatisfied after their 'problem solving' session than before it.

However, this drive home was different. This time he saw a natural Red awaiting him. And even though he tried not to analyse the situation, he couldn't help but think of how much his partner's behaviour gave her away.

She cried in movies that he saw as puerile and totally illogical. She was always the person who others confided in, and was always lending a helping hand to the emotionally frail. And boy did she get upset when he got out his calculator at the restaurant to determine how much each party owed!

Bert pulled into his driveway to see his little girl, Yasmin, waiting as expectantly as always. Usually, this sight would have Bert automatically thinking of the excuses he could make for not being able to play games with her or read her a book until after he had done some work on his home office computer. And often by the time he emerged from his office, had dinner and watched the news, it was time for her bedtime, and she would patiently go to sleep hoping that maybe next time would be different.

But this time something strange happened. Negative thoughts did not enter his mind. Instead, he made a conscious effort to ask Yasmin what she would like to do first – read a book or play games.

Yasmin was delighted, yet a little bemused. Daddy seemed different somehow. He even looked different. Not in physical features but still somehow different. Maybe it was his smile or the spring in his step. It was as though someone had lifted a huge weight from his shoulders.

Rita, Bert's wife, was even more confused when he approached her, kissed her gently and lovingly and then proceeded to ask her about the new flowers in the front garden. Then instead of retreating to his home office 'cave', he searched the bookcase for a funny children's book to read with Yasmin.

As Bert himself would later confess, this awareness of others changed everything. He was seeing Yasmin and his wife through different eyes. Suddenly, Yasmin truly was more important than work.

And his wife was not the 'somewhat less intelligent' partner in his marriage who he had to protect by handling the finances and solving all her problems. He now saw his wife as an amazing woman with strengths he admired more than any intellectual giant he had ever met.

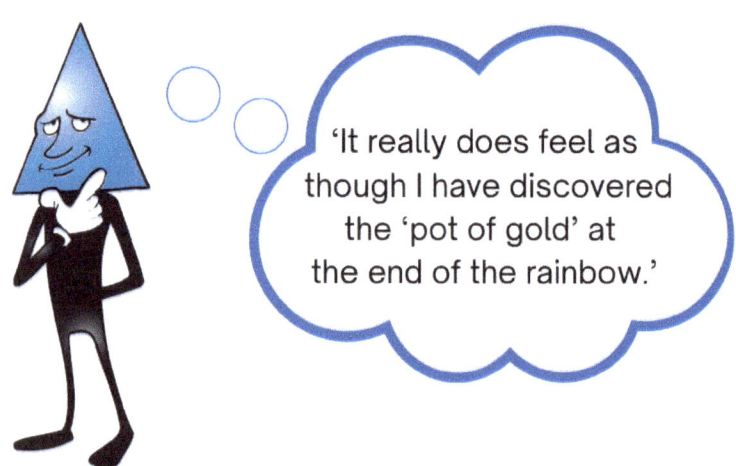

'It really does feel as though I have discovered the 'pot of gold' at the end of the rainbow.'

Yet they were the same people he had lived with all those years. And they had not changed their behaviour or outlook on life. He had changed his. And he loved what was happening.

'I love you,' he blurted out impulsively for the first time in his life. And rather than feeling embarrassed at being so 'soft and mushy', he felt elated and smiled as he looked at his family.

Rose always loved coming home after work. Home had always seemed just that – home, whereas work was always a bit cold and alien.

Even before she arrived home, the simple act of waving to her neighbours, whom she knew intimately, made her smile. And her children, Robbie and Gretel, plus her cats, Yowser and Belle, greeted her as soon as she opened the door.

Little things like the smell of her kitchen and the comfy sofa where she read her romance novels filled her with a sense of happiness.

Only boring chores like cleaning the house and doing the dishes, and the occasional frustrating phone call from her ex-husband, reduced her sense of almost spiritual bliss.

The only difference on this occasion was that her mind was filled with the expectation of being able to observe how delightfully different her children were.

Robbie is so like me, she thought. Such an obvious Red. He is so easily affected by other comments and has always loved his kisses and cuddles – even now that he was approaching the dreaded teenage years.

Yet his twin sister, Gretel, was such a Green. So tidy and organised. So careful that she didn't even fall over when she was a toddler trying to walk. Even now she would rather do something 'practical', like organise her diary, rather than talk on the phone for hours like her brother.

'I don't know if I am being too sensitive to this newfound knowledge,' Rose thought as she drove home. 'But it seems I can even describe my cats with some conviction now,' she laughed. 'Yowser shows more Yellow behaviour – very playful and always up to mischief – while Belle purposefully stalks through the house as if she is analysing the best escape route in the event of a fire.'

'There are so many ways I can use the Click! Colours.'

'My house, my castle' was always uppermost in Gail's mind every time she approached the home she had bought and renovated all those years ago. The very sight of her house instilled a sense of pride in her. And once inside her castle, simple tasks like tidying the house put Gail in an almost meditative state.

She wouldn't describe such routine, step-by-step jobs as being exciting or blissful, but the sense of achievement and restoration of order they delivered reduced the stress she felt when things weren't 'in their place'.

Living alone made this goal of having a tidy home more achievable and allowed her to spend more time in her beloved garden.

But even a loner like Gail wasn't just thinking about herself. She, too, reflected on the words of Leica Rainbow:

'No person is an island. We live with people – family, loved ones, friends, workmates, even casual acquaintances – all of whom impact on our lives and we upon theirs.'

And it was her closest friend, Bayani, that she most considered.

At first, she could not reconcile Bayani's behaviour as being relevant to the Click! Colours they had explored with Leica. Then, upon reflection, she remembered details from their last lunch. Bayani had insisted on showing Gail her latest puzzle. It was going to be Bayani's topic for her mathematics thesis at university. She was so proud, yet even a practical person like Gail found it uninspiring. But Bayani could explain, almost passionately, for hours how the equations could solve problems she might encounter when she worked as a research scientist.

The practical application of such models escaped Gail at the time, but she now realised that Bayani was simply being a natural Blue – a revelation that surprised her. She had left the workshop assuming that all Blues had to be 'cold, heartless, left-brain dominant males'. She had not even considered the complexity of left-brained females, despite the warnings about stereotypes and generalisations that Leica had repeated.

Yes, Bayani would be a very natural and comfortable Blue, she concluded. And if I were to take the risk of putting her cards in order myself, I would put her as a:

1. Blue, 2. Yellow, 3. Red, 4. Green

'Now that I understand how Bayani thinks, our relationship will grow even stronger.'

... a combination of sub-personalities which, if correct, was sure to confuse most people – and even more challenging for a natural Green who likes to have the world in order. Gail considered what she might do that annoyed or frustrated Bayani.

Yuri was excited in a way that only a natural Yellow could be. Yet, it was with a cautious note still reverberating in his mind.

'Let others become willing participants in learning about themselves. People are likely to resist if they are bombarded or confronted with new knowledge and tools, especially when the topic is themselves,' were the words he was still hearing as he drove home from the workshop.

For Yuri, home life was always just a base from which to launch out into the world. He would venture out to seek new experiences on a regular basis, sometimes to the dismay of his wife and children.

But at least when he did return, he would always be armed with some surprise: toys for the children and something special for his partner.

Yuri would have liked to have the family travel with him more often. He occasionally suggested they go with him but admitted to himself, deep down, that he was sometimes glad they didn't as it was fun being a sole explorer. He did, however, wish they would live life to the full more like he did rather than just exist like other people.

But today was different. Instead of being self-absorbed by the experience he had just undergone at the workshop, he was thinking on a deeper plane. This time it wasn't so much about his adventure – 'the journey to explore the Rainbow' – but rather how he could use his revelations to boost his relationship with his partner and children.

So, his thinking turned to wondering what their 'natural' colours and less 'natural' colours would be. 'I wonder what their Click! Colour Spectrums are, and how has that shaped our relationship?' he pondered.

'What frustrates or annoys you?'

Leica had asked this question during the workshop, and a picture of someone neatly folding towels had come into Yuri's mind.

The person in the picture was his partner, Georgina. Georgina, he surmised, must be a very natural Green. Her habit of always wanting to be everywhere early – even to doctor's appointments, which he knew would always be late – was one of his pet frustrations. Often, he would argue that they didn't have to leave the house so early. 'We have plenty of time to get there!' – be it functions or airports – he would exclaim as she insisted they leave.

She even packed her bags and the children's bags the day before their holiday, another act he couldn't understand. 'I'll pack mine in the morning,' he would retort. 'And without the need for a checklist,' he would boast, only to find that he had left his toiletries behind upon arrival. 'Never mind, I can buy some here,' he would reply when she asked him how he could have been so careless.

Yet he did secretly admire Georgina. Not only was she a wonderful partner, mother and friend, but she was also so practical. She could fix stuff around the house much better than he could – a fact he kept concealed from his male friends, whose tool shed was their second home.

He would rather be out exploring life and the big picture than fiddling with mundane tasks like gardening and tidying up the house. But then someone had to do it, he smiled to himself as he pulled into his driveway.

At home on the first night after the workshop, everyone's life remained as usual. All followed Leica Rainbow's advice and resisted the temptation to bombard others with their newfound knowledge. But before going to bed that Friday night, they all left their four coloured cards somewhere others would find them in the morning, Gail strategically placing hers next to the phone to remind her to ring her friend Bayani to arrange another lunch.

Gretel was the first to rise in Rose's household. The first thing she noticed while making her breakfast were some cards lying on the kitchen table.

She looked at them, read them and smiled. The Green card was so much like her. And even though the other cards also had aspects of her personality, it was the Green card she kept placing first in line along the tabletop. Even the way she placed the cards neatly in line reaffirmed her initial impression that the Green card was most like her, the Blue card a little like her, Red card less like her and she couldn't initially see any resemblance in the Yellow card. After placing the cards in order – again and again – and always coming up with the same sequence, she resolved to share this 'game' with her brother when he emerged from his slumber.

She didn't have long to wait as Robbie walked into the kitchen rubbing his eyes.

'Look at these!' exclaimed Gretel. 'I bet I know which colour card is like you!' she teased.

'What are you talking about?' enquired Robbie, still half asleep.

'These cards I found on the table. Have a look at the Red one. It looks like you. It's even the same colour as your pyjamas,' she beamed.

'Oh, stop teasing,' said Robbie as he accepted the cards Gretel handed him.

Immediately he was enthralled. The Red card did indeed strike a chord with him. He felt in agreement with almost everything it said.

'Where did these cards come from?' asked Robbie.

'I don't know,' replied Gretel. 'I just found them lying here on the table. Maybe they have something to do with that workshop Mum attended yesterday. Remember the one she did not want to talk about last night?'

'Yeah, but she did say she would gladly discuss it the next morning, which is now, so let's go see if she is awake,' suggested Robbie, as they walked quietly down the corridor to see if Mum's bedroom light was on.

The light was on, and Rose was reading in bed when she noticed her children standing at her doorway.

'Mum, are these your cards?' asked Robbie.

'Yes, they were used as tools at the workshop to help us explore different personalities,' Rose responded. 'Have you children been playing with them?' she asked.

'Yeah, they're kinda fun because the Red card talks a lot about things I like, and Gretel put the Green card top of her pile,' Robbie offered. 'And we both thought you were very much like the Red card because you are always so kind to us.'

'Oh, am I that obvious?' blushed Rose. 'Well now that you have found the cards, let's play with them. What behaviours do you think they explain?' she enquired, following Leica's advice.

Similar events were also happening that Saturday morning at Yuri and Bert's homes.

Yuri was actually listening to his family instead of his usual habit of just telling them things and interrupting them when they tried to speak. He was using 'Conscious Effort' (as Leica called it) to stifle his bad habits. Instead, he was using his less natural Red abilities to listen to what they were really saying, rather than automatically turning himself into the centre of attention. And although it was hard, he was enjoying the experience and noticing how much more relaxed his family were during this interaction with him. He had never considered that he could be anything but liked and appreciated. He now saw that sometimes he must have been a pain to be around. Now he and his family were laughing about how he would get annoyed if they wanted to watch the previews of next week's TV shows.

'Don't watch them; they will ruin the surprise when you see the real show. Don't you understand? What is wrong with you lot?' they said, mimicking his response to their desire for a glimpse of what they would be watching in the next episode.

'Hey Dad, now I know why you annoy me so much,' said one of his teenage daughters, holding up the Yellow card. 'You must be the biggest "Yellow" I have ever met,' she beamed. 'All those times we were almost late for my swimming training. And remember when you dropped me off at the wrong pool for one of my competitions?' she teased.

'And you know what? I am probably one of the biggest Greens you have ever met,' she continued, much to Yuri's surprise and pleasure.

'So, I must really annoy you when I keep straightening your tie and when I filed all those documents you had lying over your desk,' she concluded, holding the Green card proudly in front of her as they both laughed at themselves.

But it was at Bert's home where the 'Rainbow' was shining brightest of all. His wife, Rita, found the cards on the dining room table and had sought out Bert after pondering them for a while.

'Honey, did you leave these cards here?' she enquired.

'Yes, they were one of the tools we were given at that workshop on Friday,' he replied.

'Oh, the one you said would be a total waste of time?' she added.

'Yes, but in fact it was really good. The best one I have ever been to. A lot of people stuff as usual, but I was surprised at how useful understanding yourself and others could be,' he explained.

'I brought those cards home to share with you. I thought the information about people and personalities the facilitator covered could be just as useful at home as it will be at work,' he continued.

'I'm glad you brought them home,' Rita replied. 'Just a quick look at them explains a lot about you and me,' she beamed.

Bert bit his lip to stop himself from giving her the logical explanation for what he assumed she was about to say about the cards, and was so glad he did. Rita painted the clearest picture of him he had ever heard and was so forthcoming about herself.

'How come we never talked like this before?' asked Bert. 'I actually feel so much closer to you now and for the first time in my life I don't feel like I have to justify everything to you or anyone. I can just be myself.'

'I have tried to talk like this before with you on many occasions,' replied Rita. 'But previously it was like chasing someone over a wall and into a deep, dark cave. You would either argue that my comments weren't rational or play mind chess with me. You would often retreat to the safety of trying to problem-solve the issues rather than simply accepting what I was saying – right or wrong – then seeking to understand why it was important to me.'

'Wow!' said Bert. 'You know what? When you started speaking, my initial response was to start analysing the logic, inconsistencies, and unfairness of your words again. But I stopped and focused instead on what you were saying. You really just want me to listen and understand, don't you?'

'Yes, yes, yes,' Rita replied with a tear in her eye, as they sat together and held hands for the first time in years.

14th Piece of Gold

Understanding the Click! Colours will enhance relationships at home.

15

Use the Click! Colours to Build Quality Workplace Relationships

'We should acknowledge our differences, we should greet our differences, until difference makes no difference anymore.'

Dr Adela A Allen

Surprisingly, Bert was the most enthusiastic proponent of the Click! Colours back at work. Surprising, because the others thought he would turn up on Monday having dismissed the workshop as just another fluffy, irrelevant exercise compared to the importance of building shareholder wealth.

Instead, Bert treated the new information and tools very seriously. Whether consciously, or through some subliminal need, he realised that this could solve his most vexing problem in the workplace – other people.

Gantt charts, cost-benefit analysis, financial modelling, systems and processes alike all made sense to him. Even the workplace jargon like strategic this and strategic that, which annoyed the heck out of him, was understandable. But the behaviour of people at work had often made him frustrated and wanting to tear his hair out.

Why couldn't they see the logic behind what he was presenting? Who cared if morale was low so long as we were still profitable? Why did I constantly receive advice from others about my staff? Surely that was the job of the Human Resources department. What did people have to do with business anyway – we produced quality products and provided service for money didn't we? Why did I have to do feedback sessions with my staff? Surely, they already knew how good their performance was without me having to tell them.

But deep down he had always yearned to be liked and appreciated by the people around him – despite the numerous times he had told himself he didn't need others.

And it was this desire to 'get along' with others and for them to like, appreciate and respect him, that he saw being satisfied by Click! Colours. (Mind you, if it wasn't a logical framework, the cards may have remained in his desk drawer for longer.)

So, the first thing Bert did in his regular Monday morning meeting was to hand everyone in his team a set of Click! Colour Cards.

'Take these away, think about them, analyse them and then place them in order of priority, then fill in the blank Click! Colour Spectrum card I have given you. We will then discuss the results at next week's meeting so I can understand all of you better and you can begin to truly understand me,' he instructed the bemused group of people. Bert then sought out Regina (the person in his team who got most upset at Performance Appraisal Time). It was Regina who had become upset at his efforts to lift her from a 'B+' to an 'A' at their last meeting.

'Regina, could you please wait a minute?' asked Bert, with an unusual softness in his voice as the team filtered out of the meeting. 'Let's go and get a coffee. I'd like to share something with you,' he offered.

At first, Regina was a little hesitant – the memory of their last 'one-on-one' meeting still fresh in her mind. But Bert seemed different somehow. Even his body language was less aggressive than normal.

'Sure, I've got time before the social committee meeting at 11am,' she replied.

Bert then surprised her by leading her outside the office and across the road to a small café where he picked a quiet corner table.

'I've been thinking about our last discussion concerning your performance. You know, the one where I suggested ways you could do better than a B+,' he started, and then paused as he noticed a faint tear forming in the corner of her eye. Surely, she wasn't still upset. That discussion was days ago, he thought. If I were in her shoes, I would have simply analysed my advice and implemented the ideas that made sense. No point staying upset – just get on with it – he reasoned. Then he remembered more of Leica Rainbow's advice.

'Everybody is different. We all look at rainbows through different eyes. Some see how neatly the colours are arranged in a perfect arc (like Gail). Some think about the water droplets and how the rays of the sun are warped to produce different wavelengths of the spectrum (like Bert). Some just wonder at the exciting, vivid colours and feel lucky being able to experience such a sight (like Yuri). And some feel closer to nature and at one with the world at the splendour of it all (like Rose). Yet ALL of us can see all of these combinations to various degrees if we choose!'

This re-framed Bert's thinking. 'Regina obviously saw our discussion from a very different perspective than me,' he thought. 'So, I had better start by trying to understand where she is coming from,' he decided.

'Regina, I'm sorry about the way I jumped in and started giving you advice about how to improve last time we met,' Bert started. 'I was just trying to be helpful. I really respect you and value your input to our team, and you probably deserved an 'A' but I don't think I have ever given one in my life. My dad used to say that an 'A' meant you were perfect, and since no-one's perfect, 'B+' is the highest grade you should give as it encourages improvement,' he continued.

'But now I think he was wrong. An 'A' doesn't mean perfection. Rather, it signifies you are at the very top of the pile.' He was starting to slip back into a rational argument as he stopped himself again and offered, 'but getting back to you, Regina, tell me what you think you have been doing really well, and is there anything you think you could still improve?' he finished and gave her time to respond.

Now Regina was really surprised. This was the first time he had ever asked her what she thought about her own performance. He had on occasion asked her opinion on others in the team – something which put her in a very awkward and uncomfortable situation – but never about herself.

'Well, I may never get this chance again,' she thought, 'so here it goes.'

Gradually, Regina opened up, surprising Bert on many levels. Firstly, he realised just how intelligent Regina really was; secondly, how articulate she was; thirdly, how self-aware she was and how much she understood her performance; and fourthly, and most surprisingly, how 'hard' she was on herself. Regina was saying things about her performance that even Bert thought was a bit harsh.

It was while listening to Regina that Bert realised that most people, even natural Reds like Regina, tend to be more self-critical about their performance when they know exactly what they are trying to achieve.

 Meanwhile, back at work, Rose was much more circumspect with her cards. She simply placed them on her assistant's desk and waited for him to arrive at work and approach her.

It didn't take long after he arrived at work before he picked up the cards and walked into Rose's office, whose door was always open.

'Good morning, Yorkie,' Rose greeted him, as he strode into her office with an excited look on his face.

'Ah, I see you found those cards I placed on your desk. I left them there because I would like to hear your initial thoughts on whether we should use them with the rest of our team,' Rose said immediately, to alleviate any possible embarrassment or misunderstanding on his part.

'We used them at our workshop, and I was thinking they might be useful in helping us understand the different personalities in our team – perhaps they could help us work better as a team,' Rose continued. 'What do you think?'

'Yeah, they look like they could be fun to explore,' replied Yorkie, verifying what Rose already knew about her natural 'Yellow' colleague.

'Good, but I would like you to read and think about them first, and then come to me with a structured proposal on how we can best use them,' Rose said, watching the initial enthusiasm drain from Yorkie's face.

'But you know I'm not very good with that detailed, analytical proposal stuff they do here at Spectrum Enterprises,' Yorkie argued, as he started to subconsciously put the cards away into his pocket. 'Besides, I have too many projects happening already,' he continued.

'Yes, and when you read and fully understand ALL those cards – not just the Yellow card you are now holding – you will know why I would like you to think through what we should do with the cards in more depth. You see, stepping outside your comfort zone is one of the key learnings I would like to convey to us all,' Rose explained, as the shine returned to Yorkie's face.

'Okay, that's a challenge I accept. And you will get the best proposal I have ever produced,' he beamed, and he walked out of her office, feeling uplifted by the prospect of creating a new proposal for team growth.

Gail was laughing to herself as she caught herself straightening the pictures in her office – again. On any other occasion, her subconscious need for order would have gone unnoticed. But this time she was very much aware of her actions. But she didn't force herself to stop fussing. Rather, she allowed herself to file away documents in her in-tray but only after she had sat down and listed the Top 3 Priorities for the day.

Must Do Today	Done	Delegated
1. Explain Click! Colours to my team and give them colour cards to reflect upon.		
2. Post the Click! Colour Cards to Bayani so she can read them before lunch next week.		
3. Ask Yuri to resend his ideas about changes to the Health and Safety manual.		
N.B. Make a new list of Top 3 Priorities once I have finished this one.		

But it wasn't just the satisfaction of ticking off her 'To Do' list that made this day like no other. It was her reaction to a chance encounter that she would never forget.

Bumping into Yuri at the coffee machine, she found herself asking him if they could revisit some of the ideas he had about changing some of the safety procedures. The smile that emerged on Yuri's face continued throughout their two-hour impromptu meeting. And even though it meant Gail was running behind her schedule for the day, she felt it was the most satisfying discussion she had ever had with Yuri.

Surprisingly, some of the ideas he had about changing the emphasis to behaviour-based change rather than just rules and regulations started to make sense to Gail, especially after they talked through the practicalities of how it could be implemented.

For the first time, Gail allowed herself space to listen to what she had previously assumed were just more foolish schemes that Yuri had dreamed up. By giving him the benefit of the doubt and asking pertinent questions about how it would work in practice, she noticed herself being more drawn to his ideas. In fact, if Yuri's ideas about changing people's perception and beliefs about safety and thus their behaviours actually worked, it would alleviate Gail's biggest concern – the fact that despite her best efforts and very specific rules, regulations and detailed procedure manuals, Spectrum Enterprises still had one of the worst safety records in the industry.

Gail was elated as she hurried to her next meeting. Rarely had she been so excited about finally making a difference. And she wondered why she had let her perception of Yuri as a 'dreamer' get in the way of her life purpose of making their workplace safe for everyone.

It was then that the power of understanding yourself and others hit home. Simply accepting others for who they are rather than judging, assuming, stereotyping and reacting to differences was the key that unlocked the door to great relationships and achievements, she concluded in a flash of inspiration that amazed her.

'This is not complex. This does not necessarily require the brilliance I admire in Bert, or the creative genius that occasionally sprouts from Yuri, or even the incredible intuition that Rose displays,' Gail realised. 'Anyone can accept themselves and others and work better together if they simply understand the unique attributes of different personalities.'

What Leica had up on her final slide at last Friday's workshop was definitely true, she concluded, as she visualised the slide:

USE THE CLICK! COLOURS TO BUILD QUALITY WORKPLACE...

> **Diversity, when understood and used, creates exceptional results.**

At that same moment, in the Marketing Department, Yuri's team was stunned. Not only was Yuri on time for the regular 9am Monday team meeting (there had even been times when he had forgotten to show up at all), he was early and handed out a meeting format sheet outlining the Purpose, Agenda and Logistics.

Marketing Team Meeting

PURPOSE
1. To update results and news from last week.
2. To share upcoming events with total team.
3. To capture and assign any new actions.

AGENDA

Time	Item	Outcome	Facilitator
0900	Confirm Agenda & align expectations	Everyone is focused on this meeting	Yuri
0905	Follow up progress on previous actions	Actions completed, changed or scrapped	Yuri
0910	Update results and news	Team knows what is happening	Yuri
0920	Upcoming events	Everyone is aware of what is planned	Yuri
0930	Open forum ideas, new actions required	Detailed Action Plan Updated	Randy

LOGISTICS
Venue: Room 3.12
Facilities: Data capture remote & screen, tea, coffee, muffins.
Preparation: Read weekly report & bring any new information that needs to be shared with the team.

'Oh no, he's been to another time management course! This means we will have to play along until he gets bored with this stuff in a couple of days,' thought the team, remembering the last time the company had sent him to training. That time it had been to improve his organisational skills, and he had come back trying to change all their schedules. Some of them still had the fancy digital organiser he had given each of them – and then promptly left his own organiser gathering dust on his desk.

'Now, I know many of you are thinking that the agenda and format for this meeting are part of another fad I have temporarily adopted,' Yuri started, looking at the startled faces in front of him. 'But this time it's different,' he stressed. 'This time what I have learned is not a whole bunch of management stuff. This time I have learned about ME. And just as importantly, I am now on a quest to learn more about YOU as well. But don't look so worried. I am not going to be subjecting you all to psychological tests, or make you do silly games like in the past. This time I am simply going to help you understand yourself and others in your own time and space. I am not going to bombard you with my or anyone else's opinion. I am simply going to give you the tools and guidance to do it yourselves,' he continued.

'When we get to Item 3 on the agenda, I will be updating you on the workshop I attended last Friday,' Yuri instructed. 'And I will be giving each of you four coloured cards to take away with some simple instructions.'

'But let's leave that until later. It's now 9am, so let's begin our meeting. First item on the agenda is to remind everyone that this is just our weekly 'touch base' meeting, and more complex planning and project issues can wait until our main monthly meeting later this week.' Yuri was talking with an air of calmness and discipline that the team had never seen before.

'Maybe it truly is different this time. Maybe Yuri is serious about improving himself and us?' they pondered, as he progressed into the meeting that was the first step to a new work life.

But it wasn't just the marketing team that was stunned by the difference to what was normally a frustrating work environment. Yuri, too, was surprised by some of his team members. In particular, he was pleased with how Rod (the person he perceived as the 'least capable' member of his team) actually shone through. He was astounded at how much Rod had changed.

He had known Rod for over 10 years, and this was the first time he seemed to make sense to him. How could he have learned so much so soon, he wondered, until it dawned on him that Rod hadn't changed at all. It was Yuri who had changed.

Yuri realised that by blocking his usual judgmental thoughts, and by curbing the urge to finish Rod's sentences for him (he always assumed he knew what Rod was about to say), Rod actually made a lot of sense (even though he didn't articulate his thoughts as quickly as Yuri would have liked!).

This revelation felt weird to Yuri. Being self-aware was a totally new sensation.

Normally being busy, having heaps of new projects to start (but not necessarily finish) and being distracted by new opportunities and interests around every corner, Yuri never had time to reflect. Besides, he viewed such reflections as looking backwards and thus being negative and not future-focused.

Now Yuri realised how much he had missed out on, how much of his latent potential lay hidden by the overbearing nature of his 'Can Do' personality.

It was almost as if he had been skimming along the surface of life (albeit at a great rate of knots) and never exploring the enormous depths below. And as he reflected, he considered the significance of an old Ralph Waldo Emerson quote:

'Oh man! There is no planet, sun or star could hold you, if you but knew what you are.'

15th Piece of Gold

Understanding Click! Colours will enhance relationships at work.

16

Use Click! Colours to Improve Your Life

If behaviour doesn't change, nothing changes.

It had been 10 months since the team had attended the workshop that had changed their life. And they had almost forgotten the pledge they had made to Leica Rainbow about ongoing improvement. In fact, all but Gail were amazed that 10 months had gone so fast, and that it was now time to meet with Leica to review progress and seek further improvement.

Gail remembered because she had put the date in her diary 10 months ago. She even had reminders flagged with a warning to prepare one month prior to the follow-up session. Luckily, Gail also remembered that Bert, Rose, and especially Yuri, were not always as conscious of detail and as meticulously organised as she was, so she had also reminded them to fill out their 'Personal Awareness' Charts that Leica had given them to boost self-awareness.

Leica was beaming as she welcomed the team. Firstly, because she was glad to see them again; secondly, because they were all smiling; and thirdly, because the head of Spectrum Enterprises had told her how pleased she was with the improvement in the performance and general demeanour of all of them.

'I can't wait to share my Personal Awareness Chart with you,' exclaimed an excited Yuri, 'but I will step back and let one of the others go first so I don't always hog the limelight,' he smiled.

'Very funny,' said Bert. 'But a good idea. Let's hear from Rose first, if that's okay with you and Gail,' he suggested.

'Go ahead,' said Gail. 'We are all keen to hear your thoughts, Rose. Do you mind sharing them with us all?' she enquired, being aware that, like the others, sometimes people do not like to be put on the spot.

'No, that's fine by me,' Rose replied. 'In the past I would have been a bit embarrassed, but I think it would add value to share everyone's revelations. We are now much better at accepting and helping each other, so here goes.'

Rose carefully put her Personal Awareness Chart up on the flip chart stand – something that previously would have sent shivers down her spine – not because she would be worried about making mistakes, but more because of how it may have elicited judgmental thoughts and even comments from others.

'I have followed the format that Leica gave us and listed what I have observed as my key Strengths, possible Limitations, potential Opportunities, and Threats derived from the perceptions of others. I have also included feedback from others at work and home as Leica suggested. However, I also took the liberty of asking my parents their observations of my behaviour and personality to get a complete picture of who I am and how others see me,' she continued.

Personal Awareness Chart
How I can apply the Click! Colours to improve my life
Rose
Primary Red: Carer

Strengths that I should build upon are:
- In tune with my emotions
- Natural empathy for others
- Aware of and sensitive to surroundings
- Easy to talk to and share problems with
- Will help build harmony between individuals and in the team
- Great sounding board as I am not judgmental or a compulsive problem solver

Limitations I need to be aware of and seek to overcome are:
- Sometimes uncomfortable with the 'hard' side of life -money decisions, giving constructively critical feedback, telling friends, workmates, loved ones to back off if they abuse my kindness
- Tend to make decisions just because it feels right rather than analysing the rationale
- Tend to avoid conflict and doing things that may hurt people's feelings even if it is for the right reasons
- Sometimes too trusting rather than thinking more objectively about what I have been told or asked to do

Opportunities for growth include:
- Use my intuitive people skills 'to help others' (e.g. be more up front in offering guidance to others who may not sense the impact they are having on others)
- Leverage people and profit issues to get the best result for all e.g. when developing my people, link the interventions with Return on Investment to the company via productivity measures)
- Build upon my strengths to boost the total team's ability to understand and optimise teamwork

Threats that could limit my success could be:
- From me: The only threat I saw emanating from me was if I slipped back into my comfort zone and didn't continue to use conscious effort to continually learn and improve

- From others: The main threat comes from their perception of me being different from reality. If they perceive me to be too emotional and gullible they might not give me credit for the inner strength that I do possess!

'Well done!' they all responded, as Bert got ready to put up his Personal Awareness Chart. He was pleased with the logical format they'd been given to follow.

> **Personal Awareness Chart**
> How I can apply the Click! Colours to improve my life
>
> **Bert**
> **Primary Blue-Analyser**
>
> **Strengths** that I should build upon are:
> - Enjoy problem solving
> - Natural analyser
> - Find most maths and science topics and problems interesting
> - Good at keeping others focused on 'bottom line' results
> - Usually retain a logical mindset when faced with complex problems
>
> **Limitations** I need to be aware of and seek to overcome are:
> - Uncomfortable dealing with emotional issues
> - Often impatient with 'fluffy' people (e.g. like Rose and Yuri)
> - Tend to forget or even dismiss people issues when making my 'factual' decisions
> - Sometimes hurt others' feelings by being too blunt
>
> **Opportunities** for growth include:
> - Use my (Left Brain) analytical skills to help others make better decisions
> - Seek help (coaching, mentoring) from people with better emotional antennae than me (e.g. Rose)
> - Build upon my strengths to help the team use logic to solve complex problems
> - Help my family and work team keep the 'bottom line' in focus when making decisions so we don't get into financial strife
>
> **Threats** that could limit my success could be:
> - From me: After extensive analysis I identified a key threat as being my lack of empathy for others. But I know that if I consciously seek to understand both my own and others' emotions I will grow into an even better person
>
> - From others: Other people (apart from most Blues and some Greens) perceive me as being a bit 'cold' and 'uncaring'. And if I allow others to see me as being unemotional, I may get labelled as not being a 'team player'

'Great stuff,' Yuri enthused. He was excited because it was his turn to go next.

Personal Awareness Chart
How I can apply the Click! Colours to improve my life

Yuri
Primary Yellow-Playmaker

Strengths that I should build upon are:
- I enjoy and look forward to new challenges and projects
- I am naturally creative
- I enjoy working with others especially if it involves a new, fun project or task
- Socialising is easy for me
- I am always a great contributor of ideas

Limitations I need to be aware of and seek to overcome are:
- I am often not a good listener. I prefer to do most of the talking myself and be the centre of attention
- Like to think that I have great empathy for others but deep down tend to be pretty self-absorbed
- Often take on too many projects - most of which remain unfinished
- Have the bad habit of interrupting people and finishing their sentences for hem

Opportunities for growth include:
- Use my creative (right brain) to contribute new ideas when needed
- Help others (especially people like Gail) to step 'outside the box' to explore unconventional options and take risks
- Use more conscious control to be a better active listener (As others have said - 'You have two ears yet only one mouth')
- Help my family and work team explore the 'bigger world' and live their dreams more

Threats that could limit my success could be:
- From me: Although I see myself as perfect I recognise that this is probably my biggest threat as it may prevent me from accepting that I don't know everything, and that I need to change to improve. I also need to be more humble and accept that others (especially Gail and Bert) have good ideas as well

- From others: Others often perceive me as being like a pushy salesperson due to my enthusiasm and ability to assertively influence others. This can put up barriers to accepting me as I really am - just an excitable, fun-loving person

'Excellent stuff,' said Gail as she put up her Personal Awareness Chart, making sure that it was perfectly straight.

Personal Awareness Chart
How I can apply the Click! Colours to improve my life

Gail
Primary Green-Safekeeper

Strengths that I should build upon are:
- Enjoy organising myself and others
- Good at preventing details slipping through the cracks
- Will follow through on most things and complete tasks
- Usually very practical when dealing with people and functional problems

Limitations I need to be aware of and seek to overcome are:
- Often reject any ideas that threaten the status quo
- Uncomfortable dealing with in-depth people issues which don't seem to have any practical solutions
- Will sometimes reject and occasionally even fight against change simply because no-one has articulated a realistic step-by-step implementation plan
- Tend to avoid most risks unless some form of risk management plan is apparent

Opportunities for growth include:
- Learn to balance my conservative side (risk awareness) with a greater willingness to explore opportunities
- Use my natural tendency to organise to help my family and work teams in a more inclusive, enabling manner. I need to get them more involved so they also have 'ownership' of the task/project
- Accept many others aren't as time conscious or risk adverse as I am and that's OK when it doesn't really matter
- Help my family and work team think through the practicalities of long-term projects and how they can use processes to ensure they are completed

Threats that could limit my success could be:
- From me: My biggest threat is if I continue to resist changing myself due to the strong, stable, secure comfort zone I have built around me. Thus, I need to continually and consciously observe my own behaviour and seek to improve

- From others: Others often perceive me as being too 'picky', 'down in the weeds' and 'unimaginative', which could preclude me from influential discussions, positions and life experiences. So, I will put more focus on keeping an open mind and exploring the 'big picture'

As Gail finished, there was a collective look of satisfaction from everyone, including Leica, as they all recognised just how far they had come. And that would have concluded their ongoing improvement session, had Bert not interjected with unusual enthusiasm.

'What about helping us learn about using Click! Colours in personal relationships?' asked Bert, taking the floor. (This was a request that somewhat surprised the others, who had mistakenly assumed that he would be more interested in using the Click! Colour Cards at work as a problem-solving tool.)

'Too many marriages, friendships and partnerships are damaged or destroyed every day by people who simply do not understand each other,' he continued with unerring logic.

'Yes, and what about using this knowledge to help teachers and students understand each other and their different teaching and learning styles?' suggested Rose. 'The teachers I know would love to learn more about why they get along so well with some students and why they clash with others,' she continued.

'You two must have read my mind. I have been thinking about all the possible applications of the Click! Colours,' Gail said as she joined the chorus of wanting more. 'Here is a list of uses I came up with,' she said as she handed the list to Leica Rainbow.

> **How I can Use the Click! Colours to Make a Difference**
>
> 1. Relationships: family, work, community, social, friends...
> 2. Teamwork: sport, work, social...
> 3. Decision Making: investments, purchases, lifestyle...
> 4. Leadership: leading at work, leading my family, friends, sport, social, community...
> 5. Personal Productivity: time management, life planning...
> 6. Communication: with diverse people, cultures...
> 7. Problem Solving: work, home, community, social, hobbies...
> 8. Creativity: art, music, work projects, home design...
> 9. Parenthood: relationships with my children...
> 10. Teaching and Learning: learning styles, mine and others...
> 11. ?

'I was amazed at how many uses these tools could have,' Gail continued. 'Because at first I thought it was just about ME. Then, when we started talking about others, it kept expanding to work, home, social life and got even more interesting.'

'Yes,' Yuri chimed in like an excited chorus, 'Click! Colours can help us in so many aspects of our life,' he continued. 'But Leica, there is one more thing we would love to know... Where do we find this "pot of gold"?'

No sooner had those words come out of Yuri's mouth when he realised that he knew the answer already.

They all looked at each other and said, 'We've already found it!'

'Not only that,' said Leica smiling, 'you four have already been using the pieces of gold to make a positive difference in your lives. The pot of gold at the end of the Rainbow is the combined knowledge you have gained about yourself and others.

'The knowledge and tools I have given you are pure gold that will help you get a lot more out of life than you previously thought. Just apply the same respect, trust, understanding and tolerance you have learnt among yourselves, workmates, family, and everyone you mix with, and remember:

> Great relationships are built on mutual understanding, and great relationships are the key to success, fulfilment and happiness in life!

Silence echoed through the room as they looked at each other. They all had the same expression in their eyes: wonderment and an eagerness to continue learning. Each of them couldn't wait for the next coaching session with Leica Rainbow. But until then, they knew they had much more to learn about each other and the other people in their lives.

Each made a silent commitment to see all people through different eyes.

Checkpoint 7

Now it is time to get a complete picture of yourself. On the next page, write down what you have observed as your key Strengths, possible Limitations, potential Opportunities, and Threats that you have reflected on from the perceptions of others. You may also like to include feedback from others at work and home as Rose did for her Personal Awareness Chart.

Personal Awareness Chart
How I can apply the Click! Colours to improve my life

Name:
Primary:

Strengths that I should build upon are:

Limitations I need to be aware of and seek to overcome are:

Opportunities for growth include:

Threats that could limit my success could be:

From me:

From others:

16th Piece of Gold

Understanding Click! Colours will improve your life.

The Single Most Important Lesson

It was time to go. The 'Rainbow Team' (as they started calling themselves) were sad that this stage of the program was over, but thankful for the new insights they had gained. They all thanked Leica as they were leaving, but Gail stopped in her tracks as Leica handed her a rainbow-coloured envelope.

'Open this envelope tomorrow morning at your office meeting and I'll see you all next year,' she promised, as they departed with a hug and a wave (yes, even Bert!).

The next morning Yuri, Bert, Rose and Gail gathered for their regular monthly meeting. They couldn't wait to open the envelope Leica Rainbow had given them. Expectantly, Gail opened it as the others leaned over to read its contents. Inside was a letter. It read:

> ## The Final Piece of Gold
>
> Dear Team
>
> There is one 'final piece of gold' you must find for yourself, and it lies in the answer to this question:
>
> **What is the single most important lesson you will carry forward from this day onwards?**
>
> Please think long and hard about this question and when you have an answer, write it down below and post back to me.
>
> Kind Regards
> Leica Rainbow
>
>

All four looked at each other and resolved to do as Leica asked. They agreed to ask for input from their work colleagues, clients, suppliers, family and friends whom they had exposed to Click! Colours and then meet over lunch to scope out a reply.

Two weeks later, they replied to Leica. Their response read:

> Dear Leica Rainbow
>
> Thanks for helping us find the 'pot of gold at the end of the rainbow'.
>
> The single most important lesson is based on the realisation that positive relationships are the foundation of all success.
>
> In order to build relationships, we must first recognise that people are different, unique and complex. This diversity is a core strength of the human race. Therefore, we must seek to understand and celebrate diversity by showing tolerance and respect towards others.
>
> And the single most important lesson is...
>
> But, before we give you the answer, we'd like to thank you for taking us on an amazing journey of discovery. You have helped us find 17 pieces of 'pure gold' on our journey through the rainbow. Please turn the page to review what we have discovered, and to view the single most important lesson - the 'final piece of gold at the end of the rainbow'.
>
> Kind regards - The Rainbow Team
> Yuri, Gail, Rose, Bert

17

The Pot of Gold at the End of the Rainbow

(17 Pieces of Pure Gold)

1. Understanding people's thinking and behaviour will help you build relationships and achieve success in all aspects of your life.

2. People are different, and this diversity impacts on all aspects of life.

3. Personality styles impact on how people think, feel and act at work.

4. Personality styles impact on how people think, feel and act at home.

5. We can boost relationships by understanding why people behave the way they do (including ourselves!).

6. Our thinking and behaviour are influenced by four key sub-personalities:

- The Analyser – Our analytical, logical and problem-solving side – the Blue band in our Rainbow

- The Safekeeper – Our practical, careful and organised side – the Green band

- The Playmaker – Our curious, impulsive and playful side – the Yellow band

- The Carer – Our sensitive, spiritual and emotional side – the Red band.

7. Everyone has four sub-personalities, with some colours 'shining brighter' than others.

- Each of our four sub-personalities is equally important.

- Successful people understand how to utilise their strengths and work on their limitations.

8. There is nothing wrong with people who don't think and act the same way as we do. Our brains are just 'wired' differently, which makes us see life through our own unique 'Rainbow'.

9. Stereotyping, generalisations and inaccurate assumptions reduce our ability to appreciate and leverage diversity.

10. Our behaviour is not only influenced by personality types but also by:

- Experiences, beliefs and values
- The situations we are in
- The people we are with

Providing an environment that is conducive to all personality types will boost results.

11. How we see ourselves is not always how others see us.

There are three sides to all of us:

- The person we are
- The person we want to be
- The person people perceive us to be

The Click! Colours help us understand how people see us.

12. Knowing the makeup of our own personality helps us become a better 'whole person' by enabling us to capitalise on our strengths and work on our limitations.

13. Using the Click! Colours will boost success in many areas of life, including relationships, family, teamwork, leadership, decision making, change management, and personal productivity.

14. Using the Click! Colours will enhance relationships at home.

15. Using the Click! Colours will enhance relationships at work.

16. Using the Click! Colours will improve my life.

17. And the single most important lesson – the 'final piece of gold'… turn the page…

18

The Final Piece of Gold

If you want to know how to CLICK! with people, you need to know what makes them TICK!

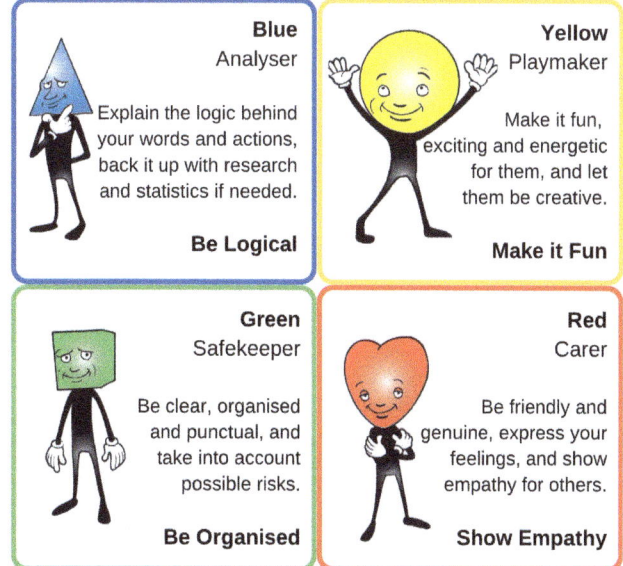

What's Next?

Congratulations! You have just taken the first step on a journey of self-discovery and understanding. The story you have just read reflects the dynamics and interplay of the different personalities that exist in every team, family and social circle. Now that you have read the story, you will start to see the colours all around you. You will see why some people CLICK! and others CLASH. And you will start to understand how you can make minor adjustments that can have a huge impact on your relationships. The more you understand what makes people TICK, the more you will have opportunities to CLICK!

This book is one step in spreading the Click! Colours message and helping others to unlock their full potential.

Become a Facilitator

If you have a passion for helping others to understand what makes people TICK, consider becoming an accredited facilitator. Our training program will give you the tools, knowledge and confidence to run your own Click! Colours workshops.

Host a Workshop

If you would like to introduce Click! Colours to your team or company through a facilitated workshop, get in touch with us or one of our facilitators. Workshops can be run anywhere, for any number of people.

Facilitator Resources

WHAT makes the Click! Colours better, faster, cheaper and easier?

The following chart summarises the key features of the Click! Colours and shows why it is a superlative tool for helping people understand and value diversity. It demonstrates why the Click! Colours are fast becoming the tool of choice for facilitators and leaders around the world who want to maximise the potential and performance of their people, teams and organisations.

The Click! Colours are **better, faster, cheaper, easier** because they are...

Useful and Usable
- Practical tool for understanding diversity
- Improve relationships, communication, teamwork, leadership and decision-making
- Suitable for workplace and elsewhere
- Very simple and easy to use
- Easy-to-understand quickly
- Affordable
- Portable
- Re-usable
- People love them

Engaging
- Fun to use
- Incorporate humour
- Generate humour
- Visual – colour, shapes, pictures
- Audio – facilitate discussion
- Kinesthetic – tactile, facilitate movement
- Print-oriented – summary cards
- Feels like playing a game
- Incorporates whole brain thinking
- Cooperative learning
- Non-threatening – suitable for everyone

Effective
- Promote sharing of learning
- Provide common language
- Reinforced by other resources e.g. posters, mouse mats,
- Use Multiple Intelligence methodology
- Change people's language and behaviour

Memorable
- Neuroscience techniques create memory hooks to embed learning
- Simple to complex - left/right brain metaphor to four quadrants to more information
- Type names describe the behaviour
- Colours are a metaphor for behaviour
- Shapes are a metaphor for behaviour
- Characters - engage and reinforce

Address limitations of existing tools
- Do not label you as one type
- Dynamic – allow you to shift with context
- Very affordable
- Take very little time to implement
- No need for questionnaires
- No need for computers
- No confusing statistics
- Easily accessible
- Easy to remember
- Very versatile- can be facilitated in many different ways and situations
- Just about anyone can facilitate them

Easy to implement
- Have memorable and repeatable 'learning bites'
- Create a common language for teams
- Highly visible
- Aligned with Jungian and neuroscience theory
- Link to other personality systems
- Resources to support implementation
- Website support
- Accreditation and training available

Products and Services

● ● ● ●

Whether you are a facilitator or hosting a workshop, the Click! Colours suite of resources includes a range of products to support and embed the Click! Colours into your team, workplace or group.

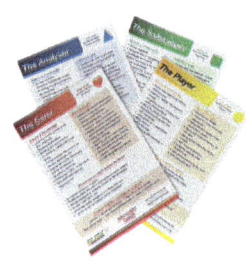

Self-Discovery Cards

The key tool that illustrates four key sub-personalities and allows people to identify the personality patterns of themselves and others. Available as A6 or A4.

Wall Charts

A set of 4 A2-size Wall Charts similar to the Self-Discovery Cards used by facilitators to run Click! Colours workshops and can be displayed in a work setting after the workshop.

PRODUCTS AND SERVICES   197

Poster

A2-size poster to use in a work setting to remind people of key messages and their colours. Useful for embedding Click! Colours in organisations and who is who.

Wristbands

Useful for workshop participants and for embedding Click! Colours in organisations.

Magnet

This postcard-sized magnet is a useful reminder of the Click! Colours in the home or at work. Perfect for embedding Click! Colours in organisations.

'Why People Make No Sense – Until They Do' Click! Colours book 2nd edition

A perfect resource for people wanting more information after a workshop, or for facilitators with tips for running their own Click! Colours workshops.

The Evolution of Click! Colours eBook

Free download from our website.

Explains how and why the Click! Colours were developed, their Unique Selling Proposition and provides a comparison to other personality tools.

For orders, bookings and more information:

In Australia: www.ClickColoursAU.com.au

Internationally: www.ClickColours.net

Cut out the Click! Colour cards on the next pages...

PRODUCTS AND SERVICES 199

The Analyser

You desire to analyse things and solve problems. You make decisions based on research and statistics as it is logical.

LEFT BRAIN TRAITS
Analytical, Logical, Problem Solving

The Analyser

LEFT BRAIN
Analytical, Logical, Problem Solving

Natural & Comfortable

- Solving problems
- Achieving 'bottom line' results
- Providing logical explanations for everything
- Using theoretical models, concepts and mathematics
- Having in-depth discussions on science and technology
- Making the 'tough' decisions
- Analysing the 'best' solution
- Taking time to make a 'measured' decision
- With technical, scientific and statistical problems

Uncomfortable

- Dealing with emotional people
- Giving personal and sensitive positive feedback
- Having to make fast decisions without the 'proper' analysis
- Discussing issues of the heart
- Being subordinate to a boss whose mental prowess does not 'command' respect
- Doing anything impulsive
- Taking 'uncalculated' risks
- Playing with 'fluffy' ideas
- With intuitive ideas/decisions

Subconscious habits noticed by others

- Often judging people — sometimes unfairly
- Tends to focus on 'cold, hard numbers' — can be perceived as 'heartless'
- Not showing emotional involvement or contributing enough of themselves to a relationship
- Incredible ability to solve complex problems in a logical manner

Possible negative perceptions by others

Unemotional • Insensitive • Lacks natural creativity • Too business-like
Too analytical • Hard nosed • Nerd • Lacks compassion

DISCOVERY CARDS

www.clickcolours.com.au
info@clickcolours.com.au

©Copyright Click! Colours® International

PRODUCTS AND SERVICES 201

The Carer

You desire to build relationships and help others. People like to share personal matters with you because you are genuine and show real empathy.

RIGHT BRAIN TRAITS
Sensitive, Spiritual, Emotional

The Carer

RIGHT BRAIN
Sensitive,
Spiritual,
Emotional

Natural & Comfortable
- Listening to other people (even their problems)
- Building relationships
- Working as a team member
- Counselling, teaching and care giving
- Having in-depth discussions on the arts, spirituality etc
- Helping others, the community and the environment
- Expressing emotions
- Discussing matters of the heart
- Non-profit and voluntary organisations

Uncomfortable
- Dealing with unemotional people (seen as 'cold, hard or uncaring')
- Giving critical feedback
- Being treated as a 'human resource' versus as a person
- Having to put the 'bottom line' ahead of workmates, customers
- Doing things which might hurt people's feelings
- Working with non-team players
- With analytical problem solving
- Working with lots of data and scientific information
- Profit above all organisations

Subconscious habits noticed by others
- Expresses emotions in public
- Trusts people to the extent of being perceived as 'gullible'
- Brings emotional or sensitive issues into the workplace
- Avoids 'hard' decisions
- Intuitively 'picks' people for who they really are

Possible negative perceptions by others
Gullible • All talk and no action • Too soft on other people
Too touchy, feely • Can't make hard decisions • Wants to save the world

DISCOVERY CARDS

www.clickcolours.com.au
info@clickcolours.com.au

©Copyright Click Colours International

PRODUCTS AND SERVICES   203

The Safekeeper

You desire clarity, certainty and timeliness. You like to make a checklist and plan things so you can be in control and be organised.

LEFT BRAIN TRAITS
Practical, Careful, Organised

The Safekeeper

LEFT BRAIN
Practical, Careful, Organised

Natural & Comfortable

- Being organised
- Being on time for everything (preferably being early)
- Putting everything in the world into its proper place
- Having everything 'in control' (especially in scheduled tasks or travel)
- Planning everything 'step-by-step' with checklists as back up
- Doing practical (hands-on) jobs
- 'Just getting things done'
- Managing and reducing risks

Uncomfortable

- Dealing with disorganised people
- Taking risks without a very good reason for doing so
- Having to look at 'big picture 30,0000ft views'
- Making last minute changes
- Being surprised by anything
- Trying new things 'for the sake of it' ('if it ain't broke, don't fix it')
- Having to strategise or dream visions
- Having to think outside of the box
- Unproven solutions

Subconscious habits noticed by others

- Too much attention to detail — can be perceived as picky
- Notes down everything in case something is missed
- Spots the little things which others might miss
- Avoids risky decisions and activities — prefers everything planned
- Likes to have everything tidy at least once a day if not more often
- Incredibly practical and self disciplined

Possible negative perceptions by others

Obsessively tidy • Bogged down in the detail • No imagination • Too detailed
Too picky • Unable to think laterally • Stuck in the 'old ways' of doing things

DISCOVERY CARDS

www.clickcolours.com.au
info@clickcolours.com.au

©Copyright Click Colours® International

The Playmaker

RIGHT BRAIN
Curious, Impulsive, Playful

Natural & Comfortable

- Taking risks (especially exciting, intuitive ones)
- Surprises, variety, new toys and change
- Visualising 'grand' schemes and selling them to others
- Being the centre of attention
- Brainstorming ideas and 'way out' innovations
- Leading teams on 'expeditions'
- Being creative
- Testing the edge
- Experimenting with new ways of doing things

Uncomfortable

- Dealing with details
- Having too many rules and boundaries
- Being asked to explain their reasoning in depth
- Being just 'another member of the team'
- Being locked into a day-to-day routine
- With 'analysis paralysis'
- Following step-by-step instructions
- With always playing by the rules
- With the status quo

Subconscious habits noticed by others

- Interrupting people by trying to finish their sentences for them
- Taking on too many projects and not being very good at the follow through
- Influencing others to get their own way
- Impulsive decision making and purchasing
- Being too easily distracted — especially by the next 'new' opportunity

Possible negative perceptions by others

Can't focus • Reckless • Too 'fluffy' • Impractical dreamer
Undisciplined • Unrealistic • Show off

DISCOVERY CARDS

www.clickcolours.com.au
info@clickcolours.com.au

©Copyright Click! Colours® International

About the Original Authors

🟡🟢🔵🔴 Greg Barnes

Greg Barnes is a well-known company director, author, corporate coach, facilitator and consultant who lives in Perth, Western Australia. Greg had been working with global organisations since 1987, and was coach to the America's Cup and World Championship yachting teams, as well as other world-class teams in both the corporate and sporting arenas.

🟡🟢🔵🔴 David Koutsoukis

David Koutsoukis is an award-winning speaker, educator, author and master facilitator who has presented at seminars, workshops and conferences throughout Australia, New Zealand, South-East Asia, South Africa, and the USA. David has a passion for the study of human behaviour and how it on impacts individuals and teams. Extensive research in this area has seen him author nine books related to this field.

About the Contributors

●●●● **Christine Kuca-Thompson**

Christine is a trainer, entrepreneur and disability ally. She has worked with government, private and for purpose organisations to support them to see each person as a unique individual with their own experiences, strengths and personalities. As a life-long learner, Christine is constantly building, designing and creating. An ideal trait to build the Click! Colours brand and resource library.

●●●● **Jennifer Than-Htay**

Jennifer is an entrepreneur, facilitator and strategist. She has run several successful small businesses, worked in the tertiary education sector, and is always looking for business trends. Jennifer is a true yellow who thrives on new ideas and different approaches. With blue being her second card, she drills down into the feasibility of her ideas. Jennifer introduced Click! Colours to the business and they use it for their own relationships as well as in the development of programs that benefit all of the colours.

Andrew Buchanan-Hughes

Andy is the owner of Click! Colours International and lives in Perth, Western Australia. Coming on as the silent partner, Andy leads Click! Colours International and has successfully introduced it to numerous organisations in Australia and facilitators overseas. Andy is a self-described 'high yellow' who loves meeting new people and sharing the Click! Colours story.

www.ingramcontent.com/pod-product-compliance
Lightning Source LLC
Chambersburg PA
CBHW061207070526
44583CB00025B/3147